VIII

What Others Say About the Book . . .

'Chris Spicer has the ability to combine the practical with the spiritual and articulate it in a most enjoyable fashion. This will be a profitable book for your library.'

> – Frank Damazio, Senior Pastor, Bible Temple,
> Portland, Oregon, USA

'A great book which, if applied, will make the difference between a successful Christian life and mediocrity.'

> – Bob Edmiston, Chairman, Subaru [UK] Ltd

'Not just theory but practical applications to everyday life, a must for every library.'

> – Dick Iverson, Founder and Chairman of
> Ministers Fellowship International

'I find the book challenging, inspiring, practical, provocative and filled with powerful, and at times, humorous and often moving illustrations. It again and again had me checking my "angle to life".'

> – Bryn Jones, Covenant Ministries International

'Chris is a good writer. The wording of his book shows that the Lord has given him much insight into the Be-Attitudes! His book reveals the living and inner spirit beyond the surface letter of the words.'

> – Kevin Conner, Waverley Christian Fellowship,
> Melbourne, Australia

VIII

Eight Characteristics of Highly Effective Christians

CHRIS SPICER

SCB Publishers

MONARCH
Crowborough

British Library Cataloguing Data
A catalogue record for this book is available
from the British Library.

ISBN 1 85424 364 0

Co-published in South Africa with
SCB Publishers
Cornelis Struik House, 80 McKenzie Street
Cape Town 8001, South Africa.
Reg no 04/02203/06

Designed and produced by Bookprint Creative Services
P.O. Box 827, BN21 3YJ, England for
MONARCH PUBLICATIONS
Broadway House, The Broadway .
Crowborough, East Sussex, TN6 1HQ.
Printed in Great Britain.

To my wife Tina,
whose love and patience,
over the years of attitude change
necessary in my life,
have made this book possible

CONTENTS

ACKNOWLEDGEMENTS

Thanks for this book must be expressed to those congregations, college students and friends who willingly listened to this material in its early days: Roger Day, David Frost, Brian Hewitt and Vicky Phillips for the hours of editorial work. Flt Lt [retired] D G Gillatt, Nigel Raymont and Rowena Hardie for their research on aircraft altitudes, peacemakers and foetal attitudes.

Appreciation must be given to Pastor Dick Iverson of Bible Temple, Portland, Oregon, USA, whose preaching on the Beatitudes first awakened my interest in the subject.

My wife, Tina and my children Esther, Hannah, Luther and Jonathan without whose love, patience, sacrifice and support this book would not have reached the printer's press.

FOREWORD

We choose our attitudes – and the choices we make have a profound impact on our life and the lives of others. So argues Chris Spicer – to great effect.

He takes his raw material from the Sermon on the Mount. Though this is well-worn territory for preachers and teachers, these words of Jesus remain some of the most quoted and least understood in history.

Thankfully, this splendid book is far more than a re-packaging of old truths in a contemporary setting. Instead it digs deeper into the life-enhancing characteristics that flow from the attitudes of those who are poor in spirit, mourn, are meek, seek righteousness, are merciful, are pure, peacemakers, and endure persecution.

The opening section, which covers the choice we all must face concerning our attitudes is a well-argued and essential foundation for all the splendid material that follows.

This book has clearly spent some considerable time in the furnace. As a result, its valuable insights are conveyed through winsome, relevant and helpful illustrations and examples.

It seems to me that the richness of these pages stems from the perceptions and attitudes of its writer. Chris Spicer does not speak of the characteristics of highly 'successful' people but rather, the characteristics of highly 'effective' people. He is wise enough to know the difference.

As a result here is a feast for those who understand – or need to – that the measure of success is not what we achieve but what we become. That God made us as human 'beings' not as human 'doings'. That our actions are ultimately decided by our attitudes.

Such a book is long overdue. I hope you enjoy it and benefit from it as much as I have.

Peter Meadows
26 June 1996

PREFACE

I have had the privilege of knowing Chris Spicer for nearly twenty years. The contents of this book are the principles by which he lives. They are not just theory but practical applications to everyday life.

I personally believe that the greatest writings of our Lord Jesus are the Beatitudes. As the author expounds on this masterpiece you will see the Christian life laid out from beginning to end and discover what makes it such a wonderful life. Every reader should heed these principles as the keys of the kingdom of God. There can be no successful Christian living without walking in the principles found in the Beatitudes of Matthew 5:1–12. I call this the 'Constitution of the kingdom of God'. This is what we base our lives upon. It is how we all walk in abundant life (John 10:10). Failure to follow these principles means a faulty Christian walk.

Chapters 5–7 are what I refer to as the 'Laws of the kingdom of God.' If we walk in the truths of these words we will find righteousness, peace and joy in the Holy Ghost (Romans 14:17).

Chris Spicer has done an outstanding job of enlarging on these principles of Christian living. It is my joy to recommend this book as a must for every library.

Dick Iverson

INTRODUCTION

'As [a man] thinks within himself, so he is.'

Proverbs 23:7 [NASB]

The America's Cup is to yachting what the Ashes are to cricket and the Superbowl is to American football. It was a bitter pill for the American holders to swallow when what they considered as 'their cup' was won from them first by Australia in 1983 and then by New Zealand in 1995.

For USA skipper Dennis Conner, the 1983 defeat was doubly difficult to take. Having gained the privilege of representing his country, Conner had committed the gravest possible offence by losing the cup for the first time in its 132-year history.

For the next four years, the defeated skipper set about restoring his country's pride and his own reputation. Conner coined the phrase 'A commitment to the commitment' and searched for ten men, from the hundreds available to him, to create a winning team.

'I made it clear,' he said, 'no one would make the team unless he put winning the cup ahead of everything else in his life. You have to start with a goal, and then put everything else aside until you achieve it.'

Seven days a week, up to eighteen hours a day, he prepared himself, his crew and his boat for the ultimate challenge.

When asked about the essential characteristics needed to regain the trophy, Conner replied, 'The three major factors in a successful crewman are *attitude, attitude, attitude*.'[1]

Have you ever noticed how some people soar above the challenges of life, while others live continually under a cloud of circumstances? Some become despondent, anxious and afraid while others take life's problems in their stride, refuse to become disorientated and somehow manage to maintain the winning edge. The reason for the contrast is simple – *attitude*.

Two brothers who are brought up in the same environment enjoying similar lifestyles can face identical circumstances. Yet while one wallows in self pity the other is able to maintain a high level of expectation in the face of all opposing factors. *The difference in approach is all a matter of attitude.*

Attitudes are those lenses through which we view the various episodes of life. They are the outlook that colours our thinking, the perception that influences the way we approach people, objects and events. Or as John Maxwell so aptly writes: 'Attitudes are the librarian of our past, the speaker of our present and the prophet of our future.'[2]

'It is no accident that some people manage to maintain a winning edge while others have resigned themselves to a life of defeat. Yet how many of us have been encouraged, let alone instructed, in the art of acquiring wholesome attitudes?'

'The longer I live the more convinced I become that life is 10% what happens to us and 90% how we respond to it,' writes Charles R Swindoll. 'This may shock you, but I believe the most significant decision I can make on a day-to-day basis is my choice of attitude. It is more important than my past, my education, my money, my successes or failures, fame or pain, what other people think of me or say about me, my circumstances or my position.'[3] Our attitude is more important than our appearance or aptitude. The fact is, a wrong attitude can make or break a company, a church or a home.

The blind hymnwriter Fanny Crosby – who wrote such songs as *Pass Me Not, O Gentle Saviour* and *Blessed Assurance* – had every reason to become bitter, lonely and frustrated. At the age of six she caught a cold causing some inflammation of her eyes. The doctor prescribed poultices that resulted in Fanny being made blind for life. Yet instead of bitterness, she monitored her thinking and chose a redemptive approach to life. It is an attitude that is apparent in some verses she wrote at the age of eight:

> *O what a happy soul am I.*
> *Although I cannot see,*
> *I am resolved that in the world*
> *Contented I will be.*
> *How many blessings I enjoy,*
> *That other people don't.*
> *To weep and sigh because I'm blind,*
> *I cannot and I won't.*

Often bedridden with consumption, Robert Louis Stevenson the great Scottish novelist and author of *Treasure Island* never allowed tuberculosis to stifle his optimism. Once when his wife heard him coughing badly, she said to him: 'I expect you still believe it's a wonderful day.'

Stevenson looked at the rays of sunshine bouncing off the walls of his bedroom and replied: 'I do. I will never permit a row of medicine bottles to block my horizon.'[4]

The Apostle Paul portrayed the same redemptive attitude. He said: 'We are pressed on every side by troubles, but not crushed and broken. We are perplexed because we don't know why things happen as they do, but we don't give up and quit. We are hunted down, but God never abandons us. We get knocked down, but we get up again and keep going' (2 Corinthians 4:8–9 Living Bible).

Escaping a life of bitterness, meaningless routine, loneliness and frustration requires the cultivating of healthy attitudes. As someone has so aptly said, 'We can alter our lives by altering our attitudes!'

Because attitudes can either hinder or promote personal development, this book looks at a theme that is fundamental to Christian life. This theme, framed around the Sermon on the

Mount, sets the standard by which all thinking is ultimately measured. I attempt to deal with the behavioural patterns that lie behind the teachings of Jesus. In so doing, I argue that our angle of approach to life is determined by our attitude. For the Christian, that approach must be *redemptive*.

But what, you may ask, is a redemptive attitude? It is the hallmark of those Bible characters who managed – some in the midst of appalling circumstances – to maintain the winning edge. A redemptive attitude could best be described as:

> An angle of approach to life whereby one is consumed by the purpose of God and constrained by the love of God to seek out, raise up and bring back people and societies which from God's perspective are lost.

Joseph refused to approach his brothers in an adversarial manner, even though they had so cruelly mistreated him. While having the power of life and death because of his position, he chose to be redemptive rather than seek revenge. Joseph, being consumed by God's purpose and constrained by his love, sought only to restore what was lost.

Daniel approached his Babylonian captivity with the same mind-set. Although he was locked into a cultural value system different from his own, he was determined to maintain a redemptive attitude and become a prophetic voice interpreting the times to a degenerating society. David's angle of approach to Saul was redemptive. So was Abraham's love for Lot, Jacob's dealings with Laban and Esther's heart for her own people. Yet these all merge into the background when we consider the life and teachings of Jesus.

'In spite of experiencing misunderstanding, ingratitude and rejection, our Lord never became bitter, discouraged or overcome. Every obstacle was an opportunity to love. Broken-heartedness? An opportunity to comfort. Disease? An opportunity to heal. Hatred? An opportunity to love. Temptation? An opportunity to overcome. Sin? An opportunity to forgive.'[5]

In Christ, the redemptive attitude is personified, for he sets the standard by which all thinking is measured.

Notes

[1] Dennis Conner, *Comeback: My Race for the America's Cup* (Bloomsbury, 1987).

[2] Adapted from John C Maxwell, *The Winning Attitude* (Nelson, 1993).

[3] Charles R Swindoll, *Strengthening Your Grip: Essentials in an Aimless World* (Word, 1983).

[4] Maxwell, Ibid.

[5] Maxwell, Ibid.

CHAPTER ONE

ATTITUDES THAT DETERMINE ALTITUDE

'Have this attitude in yourselves which was also in Christ Jesus.'

Philippians 2:5 [NASB]

'Good morning. This is your captain speaking. We have just received final clearance from air traffic control and are about to begin our approach to London Heathrow. We trust you have enjoyed your flight and apologise for any delays you may have been caused.'

As the aircraft begins to dip, passengers become aware of familiar landmarks breaking through the clouds. The River Thames shimmers in the morning sun as it snakes its way through the busy metropolis and on to the North Sea. Big Ben and the Houses of Parliament nestle neatly beside the river. The Tower of London and Tower Bridge are both clearly visible in the half light of a grey November morning.

Now into the closing stages of a well rehearsed routine, the flight crew busy themselves with the final details that precede every landing. One hostess stows what remains of an inflight meal. Others make their way up and down the sloping aisles checking that each passenger has followed the No Smoking/ Fasten Seat Belts warning signs.

As the angle of descent becomes more acute, the pilot begins to turn the aircraft towards the runway. Passengers await with a mixture of excitement and anxiety the now imminent landing. The clearly defined lights of the approach path mark the way ahead as the plane takes a sudden drop in altitude.

The relative calm of the cabin is in stark contrast to the hive of activity on the flight deck. As the aircraft maintains its incoming flight-pattern, the captain, first officer and flight engineer are faced with numerous decisions relating to their final descent. Dials and digital displays form a maze of instrumentation relaying information about the condition of the plane. In a matter of minutes the aircraft will be committed to a course of action that cannot be aborted. A wrong decision now could mean the difference between life and death.

Attitude indicator

Of all the electronic wizardry available to any pilot, one instrument is of major importance. The Attitude Direction Indicator (ADI), sometimes called the 'Master Instrument', is crucial. As a result of numerous calculations and minor adjustments, some manual, some computerised, the aircraft is aligned to the runway. The angle of descent and air speed are checked and rechecked as the aircraft draws towards the runway like metal to a magnet.

Central to the pilot's line of vision, the all-important ADI informs the flight crew of certain factors relative to a safe landing.

'But what's this got to do with human attitudes?' I hear you say.

Everything!

When I first looked at this subject of attitudes, I decided that the dictionary would be a good starting-point for my research. As I thumbed through the pages I found the appropriate section. *Attest, attic, attire . . . attitude.* I expected to discover a veritable gem of truth, and I began to read. The word 'attitude' was explained as 'the position of an aircraft'. Surely I was mistaken? I must have inadvertently read the description of the word 'altitude'.

I checked and rechecked the reference. No, it was correct; 'attitude' was clearly defined as 'the position of an aircraft'.

I realised I needed expert help and technical know-how, so I decided to call my father-in-law. As a retired Flight Lieutenant in the Royal Air Force, he would surely be able to shed some light on this subject.

Within moments, he had confirmed that the dictionary definition was correct. It appears that in every aircraft there are three imaginary lines of axis: one runs from wing tip to wing tip, another from nose to tail and the third runs vertically from the point at which the first two cross. It is on these three imaginary lines that a pilot positions the aircraft. When the plane alters its angle of ascent or descent on any of these three axes, the Attitude Direction Indicator visually records the movement. These changing angles are therefore called the 'attitude of the aircraft'; hence the dictionary definition.

Angle of approach to life

This simple but profound illustration has helped me more than anything else outside the teaching of Jesus to grasp the importance and implications of mental attitudes on our human behaviour. The basic theme of this book is to understand that an attitude is 'an angle of approach to life'. It is a concept that will thread its way through every subsequent chapter.

Our attitude is the angle of approach by which we are attracted to, or withdraw from, people, objects and events. It is the way we choose to think about things; it is our perspective on life. Maintain a wrong mind-set and the results can be devastating.

Attitudes are to life as the angle of approach is to flying. When training a pilot in the art of take-off and touch-down, the instructor will sometimes use a very simple equation:

power + attitude = performance

The same formula could be equally beneficial to the way we relate to people. No amount of energy or enthusiasm will get a

relationship off the ground if either party needs to realign or readjust his or her attitude to the other person. Success or failure in the area of interpersonal relationships is predominantly one of *attitude*. Maladjusted 'angles of approach' are often the reason why some relationships never get airborne.

The anaemic state of a marital relationship is generally the result of unhealthy attitudes. Children's inability to touch base with their parents, managers struggling to motivate their staff, employees who produce slipshod work – in many instances these can be traced to the same root cause of a wrong angle of approach.

Ted W Engstrom, commenting on certain people's approach to life, writes: 'Each of us faces people and situations every day that exasperate us. And often, despite our Herculean efforts, the exasperation simply won't go away. It's then we realise that perhaps the biggest risk of all is changing our attitude . . .

'Let me ask you a question. Do you know any grumps? I mean real bona fide grumps – the kind who frown, mumble incessantly, belittle others and walk about with a grey cloud forever hanging over their drooping heads? Not much fun to be with, are they? They are afflicted with a disease of attitude. By six o'clock each morning they already know it's going to be a lousy day!

'And then there are our friends who always seem to be "up", pleasant, interesting and interested. They are, in contrast, a joy to be around. Their warmth and good humour are contagious. They have the capacity to share their gift of encouragement with everyone they meet. Their attitudes are healthy. One of the ingredients for a life of excellence is just that – healthy attitudes.'[1]

Where do attitudes come from?

Attitudes are not innate (inborn). Neither are they accidental. They are learnt reactions, ways of responding that we absorb from parents, teachers, peers and various people who affected our early years. Our beliefs, and consequently our behaviours, are therefore the result of a process of development.

The British Museum exhibits a stone that has the imprint of a bird's foot impressed in its form. There was a time in the distant past when the stone was soft and supple, easily shaped by the circumstances of life. Now it bears the marks of a former episode in which something walked all over it.

How like people that is! Crisis, pressure and conflict can leave their mark indelibly imprinted in our thinking. As children we are very impressionable, easily moulded, marred and sometimes scarred for life by bitter experiences. All of us have grown up with various influences on our lives. Experiences, education and environment are all powerful factors that have influenced our present perspective on life – some positive, others negative.

Babies are born with a thought process that is both uncluttered and unsophisticated. Their minds are virgin soil, easily influenced. Children quickly learn to monitor and eventually mimic those attitudes with which they are surrounded. They are as susceptible to error as they are to truth. How often we have watched our children leave the safe environment of the home to attend their first days at school, only to return with a different perspective on life! The occasional swear word or unacceptable pattern of behaviour at the evening meal table all too often marks the end of childhood innocence. Yet apart from the influence of the school playground, the major player in the school of learned behaviour is still the home environment – and parents are the master teachers.

Based on a set of beliefs imbibed in our formative years, our mode of thinking forms a basis on which we build patterns of behaviour. To some degree we are all the shaped by our past. We are characterised and affected by people and events that have influenced our growing-up process.

There is a positive side to this. Through the power of spiritual rebirth and the indwelling Holy Spirit, each person can live free of these internalised restrictions. The gospel of Jesus Christ presents to us the dynamic possibility of realigning our thought patterns and shaking off the negative influences of our past.

The Apostle Paul wrote to the Christians at Ephesus: 'With regard to your former way of life . . . put off your old self, which is being corrupted by its deceitful desires; . . . be made new in the attitude of your minds; and . . . put on the new self, created to be like God in true righteousness and holiness' (Ephesians 4:22–24).

Rather than apportion blame on parents, the church or today's society, each of us must take full responsibility for our own attitudes. We need to acknowledge and then adjust any wrong thinking we may have. Like the Corinthians, we must align our thinking with God's in this way, 'we demolish arguments and every pretension that sets itself up against the knowledge of

God, and we take captive every thought to make it obedient to Christ' (2 Corinthians 10:5).

Component parts

If the secret of a successful life is in monitoring and maintaining a healthy mind-set, what are the parts that make up an attitude? The answer is simple. All mental attitudes have three main components: belief, effect/feeling and action. As such, these three elements cover almost everything we think, feel, say or do. What I believe about a person, object or event will predetermine how I feel, and how I feel affects my course of action.

Beliefs/facts

Beliefs are based on facts, generalisations, prejudice, stereotypes, experience and assumptions. They form the basic component of an attitude and become the key factor in determining and changing attitudes. Change a person's beliefs and you will undoubtedly change his or her behaviour.

The mind is a fortified stronghold that incorporates countless arguments, theories, prejudicial ideas and fantasies. All these help to predetermine the way we approach any given situation and our response to it. The English word 'believe' comes from an Anglo-Saxon word that means to 'be-live'. Under the inspiration of the Holy Spirit King Solomon put it this way: 'As [a man] thinks within himself, so he is' (Proverbs 23:7 NASB). In other words, our life is the sum total of our thoughts and thought processes.

The mind, formed during the passage of time, has created certain 'frames of reference'. These are best described as: 'Internalised learned patterns of thinking, against which a new incoming experience is measured.' It is these well-established fortifications that create a formidable opponent for any new thoughts and ultimate change of behaviour. This is clear from

J B Phillips' paraphrase of 2 Corinthians 10:5: 'Our battle is to break down every deceptive argument and every imposing defence that men erect against the true knowledge of God. We fight to capture every thought until it acknowledges the authority of Christ.'

Beliefs are therefore the basic component of an attitude. What we believe as factual [whether it is actually true or not] affects the way we act or react. Beliefs predetermine a favourable or unfavourable response to people, objects or events. In his book *How to Develop a Positive Attitude*, Elwood Chapman speaks of an attitude as a type of mental camera lens.

'Think of attitude as your mental focus on the outside world,' he says. 'Like using a camera, you can focus or set your mind on what appeals to you. You can see situations as either opportunities or failures. A cold winter day as either beautiful or ugly. A departmental meeting as interesting or boring. Perception – the complicated process of viewing and interpreting your environment – is a mental phenomenon. It is within your power to concentrate on selected aspects of your environment and ignore others. Quite simply, you take the picture of life you want to take.'[2]

Based on the facts available to us, be they true, false or invented, we all formulate certain attitudes. A rumour can be true or false, but if we give it room in our thought process it will angle our approach accordingly. For instance, if like the ancient mariners we believed the world was flat, and to venture too far from the shoreline was to run the risk of falling off the face of the world into oblivion, we would never lose sight of the coastline!

Each of us has a 'set of beliefs' concerning life. Built up over a period of years, they are the result of various environmental, educational and experiential influences. If you grew up in a negative environment, being continually told you would never amount to much, the likelihood is that those words will have created a set of beliefs about yourself in which you find it difficult to see yourself as a winner. With such a negative approach to life, every new venture is perceived as being thwarted with problems and viewed as a probable disaster.

An inadequacy to enter into the dynamics of Christian life is often rooted in a devaluation of our position in Christ. This inability to see by faith our redemptive worth in and through the risen Christ – as reflected in the mirror of God's Word – cripples spiritual effectiveness. If we choose to reflect on the negative and make wrong comparisons, we envisage ourselves as misfits having little use in God's eternal purposes.

Winners are people who have learnt to maintain high levels of expectation in the face of all-opposing factors. Abraham 'refused to allow any distrust of a definite pronouncement of God to make him waver. He drew strength from his faith, and, while giving the glory to God, remained absolutely convinced that God was able to implement his own promise' (Romans 4:20–21 J B Phillips). Choosing a set of beliefs concerning himself based on what God said, Abraham became one of life's great achievers.

Effects/feelings

Facts, when sown into a fertile mind, seldom remain as inactive knowledge. As they germinate in the ground of personal insecurities, facts produce either favourable or unfavourable feelings towards people, objects and events. We develop likes or dislikes that cause us to respond positively or react negatively.

Yet feelings on their own cannot be trusted. They are as unstable as water, fluctuating according to our mood, state of health and external conditions. They are learnt through first- or second-hand experiences and become our very own personal lens through which we view life. They provide a perspective that can change according to mood swings, circumstances, traditional values or cultural, educational and family bias.

For instance, it is possible to prejudge a stranger solely on the beliefs created through the words of a third person – be they true or false. This prejudgement produces a crop of feelings towards the individual that may or may not be grounded in reality. Racism is a classic example of this kind of prejudicial thinking – an unhealthy attitude built on a wrong set of beliefs.

Feelings therefore form the pivotal point in the three component parts of an attitude. They can be produced by beliefs or become the result of our actions. For instance, when God rejected Cain's sacrificial offering, Cain became angry and 'his countenance fell'. In response, God told him: 'If you do well, will not your countenance be lifted up?' (Genesis 4:3–7 NASB). Cain's behaviour had a direct bearing on those feelings mirrored in his facial expressions.

In the same way, a Christian – being someone who has chosen to live under God's reign of 'righteousness', that is, being and doing what is right – must recognise that a righteous lifestyle results in an atmosphere of 'peace and joy in the Holy Spirit' (Romans 14:17).

Actions

If left unchecked, our beliefs produce a crop of feelings that in turn cause a chain reaction of either positive or negative actions. Someone has aptly said: '10% of life is what happens to me; 90% is how I react.'

King David wrote: 'Let the words of my mouth and the meditation of my heart be acceptable in thy sight, O Lord, my rock and my redeemer' (Psalm 19:14 NASB). The Hebrew word for 'heart' also means mind, will and emotion or feelings.

Sadly, David failed to live according to his own code of practice. He wrongly believed that he himself was exempt from battle 'at the time when kings go off to war' (2 Samuel 11:1). In that situation David allowed his feelings for another man's wife to get out of control. Eventually his desire for Bathsheba led him into a series of events that tragically resulted in an act of adultery and then murder.

What I believe affects how I behave. You can send an army of advisers to teach Third World countries the economic and social benefits of birth control. But without the removal of ethnic barriers and religious beliefs the whole exercise proves futile. The United Nations can continue to set itself up as a self-appointed protector policing the territories of what was once Yugoslavia, but unless it finds an answer to the entrenched beliefs of both the Bosnians and the Croatians, the senseless killing will continue.

Once triggered, beliefs and feelings have a domino affect on our social conduct. With the resurgence of neo-Nazism in Germany, anti-Semitism in Poland and anti-immigration parties in Austria and Switzerland, it seems that blatant racism is back. A combination of inferiority and superiority have spawned in these nations a rebirth of resentment. It is a hatred vented on certain ethnic groups which are seen in some cases as the root cause of economic hardship. These beliefs have set off a chain reaction of resentment and violence.

The jury is out

Attitudes will cause us to react and behave in a certain way. They are our perspective on life, the metre-stick by which we size up people, objects and events.

My attitude is my angle of approach, a mode of thinking – a mental posture I adopt when approaching things. Attitudes are like magistrates sitting in judgement on the events of life. They are silent observers who look at and listen to life's circum-stances, poised to bring judgement at any said moment. Attitudes are those lenses through which we view things. As a result, they affect our perspective on life.

I had just finished my Bible college training and was still very wet behind the ears theologically. Why, I wondered, did young Peter behave the way he did? A pleasant five-year-old, he persistently hid behind his mother whenever I tried to hold a conversation with his parents. When I visited their home I would enter the front door only to see young Peter making a speedy exit from the room. He wouldn't reappear until long after my departure.

It wasn't just a bad dose of shyness; it seemed that I was the only one he treated in this manner. I tried every way I knew to establish some level of friendship with Peter, but to no avail. I had to find out who had the problem, him or me. At the end of one Sunday morning meeting I decided to confront the issue. I drew his parents aside and broached the problem of 'Peter's pastoral phobia'.

'Excuse me for asking,' I enquired, 'but could you tell me why it is that your son reacts the way he does whenever he sees me?'

'Oh,' his father replied. 'Don't worry about that. It's just our Peter.'

'But I'm concerned,' I continued, 'and I'd like to resolve this issue once and for all.'

'Well,' said his mother, feeling somewhat embarrassed and a little ashamed, 'every time Peter's naughty we tell him that if he doesn't behave, we'll lock him in the cupboard and send for the pastor.'

There was my answer! No wonder the lad behaved the way he did. He viewed me as punishment personified, the ultimate threat used by two parents unable to bring the right kind of correction to their five-year-old son. Peter had been fed certain information through which he had formed a set of beliefs. These beliefs triggered strong feelings which in turn became a driving force that caused him to take evasive action.

Like the gearbox of a car, attitudes engage human potential

to take action – progressive or regressive, favourable or unfavourable.

I heard recently about an elderly couple who decided to visit the USA. As it was their first time out of their native Yorkshire they were keen to learn from other people's experiences during their holidays abroad. On hearing that their trip included a first night stopover in New York, their friends warned them about the dangers such a city could offer. They told stories of murder, mugging and mayhem. Even before the couple's first night on American soil, such so-called 'facts' had set off a chain reaction of fear in the two apprentice globetrotters.

Once they arrived in New York they settled themselves into their hotel room and decided to go and view some of the sights. When they reached the hotel lobby, the lady realised she had forgotten her handbag. 'You carry on, and I'll go back to the room,' she said to her husband. She retrieved her bag from the room, and began to make her way back to the hotel entrance.

She entered an empty lift and was joined by a tall, handsome man with a very large dog. While trying hard not to notice these fearful-looking occupants, one very nervous lady watched as her only way of escape closed automatically in front of her.

The silence and the slow descent of the lift seemed almost unbearable. With every passing floor the tension grew. Now the dog was becoming restless, 'Why didn't I heed those warnings and avoid New York? Why didn't I stay in my native Yorkshire village?' she thought.

Suddenly, the silence of the lift was shattered by a shout.

'Get down, lie down – on the floor.'

The elderly lady dropped to the floor, sensing the worst. What she had feared most was surely about to happen. At any moment her assailant would begin his awful attack.

What she hadn't realised was that the words of command were actually meant for the dog and not for her. Almost immedi-ately one very friendly, apologetic and somewhat amused gentleman helped the lady to her feet. Apologising for the mis-understanding, the young man helped her on her way.

When the couple came to check out of the hotel, they found that their bill had been paid and the unknown man in the lift had left a bouquet of flowers. It was singer Lionel Richie's way of apologising while at the same time saying thank you for the most amusing incident he had seen in a long time!

Attitudes are made up of beliefs, which in turn create feelings that result in either a positive or a negative course of action. They have to do with an individual's readiness to respond to people, objects or events in a set way. It is the mental and some-times physical posture we adopt when approaching circum-stances.

Put another way, attitudes are predetermined patterns of thinking that affect the way we act or react to a given situation. Faced with the same set of circumstances one person will act in one way, while another person might act totally differently.

It's all a question of attitude.

Notes

[1] Ted W Engstrom, *The Pursuit of Excellence* (MARC, 1988).
[2] E N Chapman, *How to Develop a Positive Attitude* (Kogan, 1988).

CHAPTER TWO

ALL CHANGE!

'Do not be conformed to this world . . . But be transformed (changed) by the [entire] renewal of your mind – by its new ideals and its new attitude.'

Romans 12:2 [AMPLIFIED BIBLE]

Understanding what makes an attitude is one thing; what most of us want to know is: 'How can we challenge and ultimately change wrong thinking? How do we alter an attitude?'

Attitude change

Attitudes are fixed and enduring and therefore not easily changed. Like an old jacket they have become comfortable and familiar to us. To change our attitudes not only means admitting we are wrong, but it involves our having to do something, to work, to make an effort.

In order to remove the external effects of an attitude, we must first deal with our deep-seated beliefs. It is in the area of our thinking that all attitude problems are resolved. Alter a person's mind-set, and you will engage a process of effective change that will transform a negative thought pattern into a positive one. I'm not speaking here of the power of positive thinking. Neither am I teaching a kind of metaphysics of mind over matter. There is, of course, only one power sufficient to change all deep-seated attitudes – the gospel of Jesus Christ.

But what exactly *is* this power and ability that can instigate such a life-changing process? The Word of God. I know of no other instrument more able to penetrate the thick skin of human resistance and bring change. God's Word can cut through the scar-tissue of past experiences and bring healing. It can lay an axe to our wrong beliefs and instil new ones. 'The Word of God is living and active. Sharper than any double-edged sword, it penetrates even to dividing soul and spirit, joints and marrow; it judges the thoughts and attitudes of the heart' (Hebrews 4:12).

It is the application of divine truth to our lives that will bring a lasting remedy to wrong attitudes.

Own up – it belongs to you!

Earlier, I made a sweeping generalisation that attitudes determine our perspective on life and affect our approach to people, objects and events. It is equally important to be realistic about their effect on us personally. When we acknowledge wrong attitudes it is a decision of our will. We have a tendency to justify ourselves or rationalise the situation. 'I can't help it; it's my temperament,' or, 'It's not my fault; my parents were just the same.' Such efforts are not the basis for our release.

The first step to implementing change is to admit that we ourselves are responsible for our unhealthy thinking. We need to acknowledge that these attitudes belong to us and therefore cannot be blamed on others. We have to be responsible for our own deep-seated mind-set, otherwise the whole process of change becomes protracted and painful. Bob Mumford comments: 'If we decide early in the game that we are going to embrace truth whenever we meet it, no matter what the cost, we will find it much easier to deal with each test as it comes along. Buying truth on the instalment plan is always more expensive.'[1]

The person who hates authority often accuses others of being authoritarian. The truth of the matter may well be that the individual concerned has an attitude problem because of a strict disciplinarian upbringing.

It's a bit like the old lady who rushed out into the garden on a warm summer's day, frantically retrieving her washing from the line before the threatened storm. Soon she hung it all out again when she realised she had been wearing her sunglasses. 'Everything looked so dark,' she said, 'I was certain it was about to rain!' Like her, we often react to situations in a certain way because of our perspective on life.

The Apostle Paul encouraged the Philippian believers to exercise the same 'attitude' that he himself showed. He wrote: 'All of us who are mature should take such *a view of things*. And if on some point you think differently, that too God will make clear to you' (Philippians 3:15). The New American Standard Bible translates the same verse as: 'Let us therefore, as many as are perfect, *have this attitude*; and if in anything you have a different attitude, God will reveal that also to you.' Attitudes are our personal perspective, the lens through which we see the episodes of life. As such they affect the way we act or react.

Take a risk – be radical!

The Bible teaches that the basic key to all behavioural change is repentance. Since most emotional and behavioural problems issue from unhealthy attitudes, it is futile to try to treat the behavioural symptoms without dealing with the cause. It's like taking the bulb out of the car dashboard so as to deal with the problem of the flashing oil-warning light.

Biblical repentance needs a change of thinking, which in turn results in a change of behaviour. It means that we begin to view the issue from God's perspective and behave accordingly.

The prodigal son's way back to a right relationship with his father began when 'he came to his senses' (Luke 15:17). In the same way, salvation is a restoration of the whole person, a coming alive to God that begins with repentance and brings us into a wholeness of life. The prodigal's return resulted first and foremost in a restoration of his *identity*. His father's gift of 'the best robe' (Luke 15:22) was a mark of reconciliation and a means of recognising him as a son, not a servant. The son returned home feeling thoroughly condemned, locked into a devalued view of himself. The best he could hope for was servanthood. Instead, he received a public recognition of sonship.

New birth re-establishes the repentant individual to the position of a right relationship with God the Father. The indwelling power of the Holy Spirit enables people to reflect on who they are in Christ Jesus – sons of God who serve him willingly.

The speedy response ordered by the father not only restored the prodigal's estimation of who he was, but also reinstated his birthright – his *authority*. The father publicly recognised who the prodigal was. He wanted his son to understand the privileges that result from sonship.

In the Old Testament, Pharaoh had given a restored Joseph 'his signet ring . . . [and] dressed him in robes of fine linen' (Genesis 41:42) to signify the authority vested in him. In the same way the prodigal's father established the fact of sonship and emphasised the truth of a vested ability to exercise power and authority by putting a ring on his hand.

This issue of attitude change involves not only a recognition of who we are in Christ Jesus but also of our God-given rights to exercise power and authority. As sons, we have a right to rule – the power to rule ourselves as well as our circumstances. We have the ability to live free from unhealthy beliefs that lead to wrong behaviour.

With a restored sense of identity and authority, the prodigal was also given a new direction, a new *destiny*. The haphazard, aimless drudgery that hallmarked life on the pig farm was not the destiny to which he had been born. Neither is it the kind of lifestyle that God has in mind for those who are born again into the household of faith. The Damascus Road experience caused Saul to ask two fundamental questions: 'Who art thou, Lord?' and 'What wilt thou have me to do?' (Acts 9:5–6 KJV). To the

Christian the gospel of the kingdom is an issue of lordship as well as a challenge of ownership.

Acting on information received

Peter writes: 'His divine power has given us everything we need for life and godliness through our knowledge of him who has called us by his own glory and goodness. Through these he has given us his very great and precious promises, so that through them you may participate in the divine nature and escape the corruption in the world caused by evil desires' (2 Peter 1:3–4).

By receiving God's Word in faith, we are able to align our thinking with God's thoughts. Just as a soldier puts on his helmet as protection from the coming battle, so the Christian is to apply the truth, not merely appreciate and acknowledge it. In donning what Paul terms 'the helmet of salvation' (Ephesians 6:17) we appropriate God's truth to our thought process and align our thoughts with his.

Putting the same principle another way, Paul writes to the Christians in Rome: 'Count yourselves dead' (Romans 6:11). Another translation puts it, 'Reckon yourselves dead.' What is he saying? Simply this: 'Reckon on the fact that you have died to the past, and live accordingly.'

The word 'count' or 'reckon' is an accountancy term that means to realise in reality what we have available to us. Although my accounts books may say one thing, it is what is in reality available to me that counts. This involves the actual hands-in-the-pocket scenario; I literally count the money I have to use, and I live according to what is available to me. I live by the reality of facts, not feelings or wishful thinking.

Count on the fact, says Paul, that Christ has died and that you died with him. It is an historical, eternal and present fact that cannot be altered. 'He died to sin [ending his relation to it] once for all, and the life that he lives he is living to God – in unbroken fellowship with him. Even so consider yourselves also dead to sin and your relation to it broken' (Romans 6:10–11 Amplified Bible).

The redemptive work of Christ is a truth to be applied, not merely admired. We do not live freely by the so-called power of positive thinking, or the repeating of empty phrases, or a mere mental assent. Instead, through Holy Spirit revelation we build our lives on divine truth established in our innermost beings. Paul wrote to the Christians in Rome: 'We know that our old self was crucified with him' (Romans 6:6). Each of us needs to appropriate the truth, 'and the truth will set [us] free' (John 8:32).

Breaking the mould

Breaking the habit of a long-established attitude is a very real possibility through Christ. The mind-set that refuses to move beyond those old, well-worn tracks of past hurts will hinder our individual progress en route to attitude change. We need to experience the renewing power of the Holy Spirit, break out of the past and live in the fullness of God's today. We are responsible and accountable for having a resolve to alter and bring adjustment to our thinking where necessary and so align our thoughts with those of God.

If we deny all knowledge of our actions or reactions we are like ostriches, burying our heads in the sand. We are each answerable for our actions and we must therefore own our attitudes. It is no excuse to blame our behaviour on past experience, parental upbringing or peer pressure. A born-again child of God has what it takes to overcome every historical hindrance and to live victoriously. We need only engage the indwelling power of the Holy Spirit to help us mirror ourselves in the truth of God's Word and break free from the wrong images we hold of ourselves.

The little-known Old Testament character, Jabez, was branded with a name that sounds like the Hebrew word for 'pain'. Who can tell what disabling effect such a name had on his early childhood?

Words have an immeasurable effect, especially on young minds. Negative words have a crippling effect on people, emotionally and socially. Tragically, parents today still name their children with little thought as to their future. What an agony it must have been for children to grow up in the 20th century with names like John Will Fail, Welcome Baby Darling and Justin Pink! Other children, through no fault of their own, have become emotionally disabled through the jibes of a unwise parent.

Jabez, in contrast, refused his mother's indictment. He called on God to break the mould: '"Oh, that you would bless me and enlarge my territory! Let your hand be with me, and keep me from harm so that I will be free from pain." And God granted his request' (1 Chronicles 4:9–10).

No limitation was going to inhibit this man of God. He broke out of his mother's frame of reference, took hold of his inheritance and became a winner.

Cabbage-patch mentality

Paul challenges the Romans: 'Do not be conformed to this world . . . But be transformed (changed) by the [entire] renewal of your mind – by its new ideals and its new attitude – so that you may prove [for yourselves] what is the good and acceptable and perfect will of God' (Romans 12:2 Amplified Bible). The Greek word translated as 'transformed (changed)' is also used to describe the transfiguration of Jesus in Matthew 17:1–13. And in 2 Corinthians 3:18 it speaks of the spiritual process by which the Christian is 'being transformed into [Jesus'] likeness with ever-increasing glory, which comes from the Lord, who is the Spirit'.

From this Greek word we get the English word 'metamorphosis'. To the entomologist the word conveys the transformation of a caterpillar through the chrysalis stage into a beautiful butterfly. Through the process of metamorphosis the insect changes not only its form and appearance but its habits and way of life. The same can be said of those who profess to be living under God's rule (see 1 Corinthians 6:9–11).

If the butterfly is to move from its former cabbage-patch existence and survive in the totally new environment for which it is now well suited, it must change its angle of approach to life.

Through the cross of Christ we have been changed, are being changed and will be further changed. But if this middle ground of 'being changed' is not to become a quagmire of mediocrity, we need to think differently.

God has fitted us to fly, to 'reign in life through the one man, Jesus Christ' (Romans 5:17). We are to live above our circumstances, not beneath them, and we are to rule in life knowing that 'God raised us up with Christ and seated us with him in the heavenly realms' (Ephesians 2:6).

If you want to find a new formula for life that will take the hassle out of home life and the drudgery out of work, then develop a right attitude. Focus your thinking on godly ways and fix your mind on whatever is true, noble, right, pure, lovely and admirable (Philippians 4:8). Such thinking creates a wall, a protective barrier of peace that will maintain your joy as well as guard your life.

Someone once said: 'It's not that Jesus needs to do any more for us, but he does have to do a lot more in us.' This is what the Bible means 'transformed by the renewing of your mind' (Romans 12:2). Another version puts it: 'Don't let the world around you squeeze you into its mould, but let God remake you so that your whole attitude of mind is changed' (J B Phillips).

Attitude change is the result of the Holy Spirit's interacting with our spirit, changing our beliefs in line with God's way of thinking. It is therefore how you respond to God's grace in your life that makes potential attitude change possible. Here are a few keys for you to adopt when considering a change of attitude:

- Humble yourself – James 4:6–10; 1 Peter 5:5–11.
- Draw near to God – Hebrews 4:16.
- Ask for help.
- Resist negative thoughts.
- Don't buy the lie – 2 Corinthians 10:4–5.

- Put yourself under the authority of God's Word.
- Meditate on God's positive attributes.
- Apply the truth – Ephesians 6:14; Matthew 4:1–10; 1 John 4:4.

Giving birth to the new me

Any midwife or mother-to-be knows the importance and implication of a change of attitude. The position of a baby prior to delivery is known as the 'foetal attitude' and is vitally important to the birth process. The angle at which the unborn child presents him/herself determines the degree of ease which both mother and child will experience during birth.

The implications of a so-called 'bad attitude baby' are well known. Any deviation from what is termed normal can result in a difficult labour. An abnormal attitude can sometimes obstruct the process of labour. Although the majority of 'bad attitude babies' change their angle of approach unaided and so enter the world normally, those who maintain a bad attitude increase the risk of trauma to both themselves and their mothers.

We may have high hopes and great ambitions for our future, but unless we maintain a right attitude we will have difficulty in bringing to birth the vision and we run the risk of aborting the dream. Because of a wrong attitude, Solomon had the kingdom torn from him (see 1 Kings 11:11). Through 'a different attitude' (Numbers 14:24 Good News Bible), Caleb, along with Joshua, managed to achieve his goal in life. Shouldn't we also want to monitor and maintain a healthy attitude so as to fulfil our God-given destiny?

All change

As I introduced the visiting lecturer that chilly October morning, I had no idea of the incredible life story of this humble, unassuming South African. Yet for the next five hours he was to hold the student body spellbound as he told of his involvement in recent developments in southern Africa.

A white man with an impeccable Afrikaner pedigree, Dr Nico Smith had been brought up to believe that black people were dirty and inferior. Having secured a prestigious post at the University of Stellenbosch, he began to question many of his ingrained beliefs. He realised he had a mind infected by the whole concept of apartheid theology. As such he believed separation was not only right but actually beneficial to the black population of South Africa.

This racist mentality is epitomised in a story Dr Smith tells. A fellow Afrikaner was concerned about a crisis that had arisen at home. His gardener had just died and he didn't know what to do with the body. He phoned to ask Nico Smith what he should do.

'Has he got a wife?' asked Nico.

'I don't think so,' said the man.

'Well, then, you must get in touch with his relatives.'

'I don't know who his relatives are.'

'Where did he come from? Where did he go when he went home on leave?'

'I don't know.'

'What was his family name? That might help.'

'We always called him Johnnie.'

Finally, Dr Smith asked, 'How long was he working for you?'

'Forty years,' replied the man.

Challenged by this kind of ingrained racist thinking, Nico Smith knew that he had to give a biblical basis for his beliefs. As he searched the Scriptures for an answer, the truth gradually began to dawn.

'My attitude to blacks,' he realised, 'had not been governed by biblical principles at all, but by a strong sense of national identity and a fear that if the races intermingled, my identity would be threatened.'

Speaking later of this painful period of change and its challenge to his apartheid theology, he added: 'When I discovered how bad, how evil, that was, I began to look into my own personality to discover the roots of such an attitude. I came to realise that it wasn't just me, but that I was part of a whole civilisation that had developed an arrogant and aggressive attitude, a ruler mentality that sought to dominate.'

Nico Smith shocked many people by turning his back on what was considered the 'norm' among his peers. He set up home in the deprived and depressed South African township of Mamelodi. In doing so, he became, as far as he knows, the first Afrikaner ever to live in a black township. Here he experienced some of the worst violence seen in South African townships for some years.[2]

What was the reasoning behind such a course of action? Without wanting to over-simplify a very costly step, we could describe it as a change of attitude.

Notes

[1] Bob Mumford, 'Below the Bottom Line', *New Wine Magazine* (November 1978).

[2] Told by Rebecca de Saintonge in *Outside the Gate*, (Hodder & Stoughton, 1989).

CHAPTER THREE

A DECLARATION OF DEPENDENCE

'Because my servant Caleb has a different attitude . . . I will bring him into the land which he explored, and his descendants will possess the land.'

Numbers 14:24 [GOOD NEWS BIBLE]

Any incoming government that wants to introduce social, fiscal, spiritual or political reform must first find a way to alter the attitudes of its constituents. Although legislation might create the right environment for change, only a shift of thinking will ultimately change people's social behaviour.

Jesus entered this time-space world as heaven's elected representative. He came not only to extradite humanity from the ravages of sin, but also to re-establish the rule of God in the lives of earth's constituents. Through his sinless life, vicarious death and triumphant resurrection, Jesus restored to humankind the ability to do right.

Matthew 5–7, commonly known as the Sermon on the Mount, is a description of the character and conduct of God's alternative society. This inaugural speech, which could easily be called 'The Manifesto of the Kingdom', sent shock waves through the corridors of religious power by declaring God's incoming government.

Jesus prefaced his sermon with eight statements known as the Beatitudes. They describe the Christian's angle of approach to life.

Like the Ten Commandments, the Beatitudes can be divided into two groups. The first four deal with people's relationship to God, the second four with people's relationship to people. Those who have first learnt *to rely on God* by maintaining the spiritual high ground are best suited to *relating to the needs of others*.

Step by step these eight redemptive attitudes challenge every aspect of human behaviour. Together they represent the character and conduct of a true disciple.

Bat-of-the-eyelid goals

John Naber, US high school swimming champion in backstroke, was in his first year when he watched Mark Spitz achieve seven gold medals in the 1972 Olympic Games. Naber immediately set himself a target of winning the gold medal for the 100-metre backstroke in the 1976 Games in Montreal.

The difference between his personal best and the world record was five seconds – an enormous amount of time in a race of that kind. What Naber needed was a strategy – a long-term goal with short-term benefits. Having worked out that he only had to improve by one twelve-hundredth of a second for every hour spent training, he divided the five seconds into minuscule measurements of time. These 'bat-of-an-eyelid goals' became achievable targets for him to aim at.

To help map his progress, Naber covered the four walls of his study with a four-year training plan. Each wall representing a twelve-month training target. Then, with great fortitude and determination, Naber set about his goal – five seconds in four years.

Eventually John Naber was chosen to captain the US swimming team. He went on to win the 100-metre backstroke in a new world record of 55.49 seconds – 3.21 seconds faster than the previous record. In doing so, he achieved his ultimate goal, an Olympic gold medal. Step by step Naber pursued a destiny which he knew he had the potential to achieve.

Before us are eight attitudes, a way of thinking which represents a godly mind-set. Although they are the ultimate goal, they represent for those who 'participate in the divine nature' (2 Peter 1:4) a present reality. These attitudes are not an impossible dream or a figment of the imagination. They are not mere natural tendencies, present in some and absent in others. Instead, they are family characteristics that are to be naturally evident in every born-again child of God. They are our 'bat-of-an-eyelid goal' for which God 'has given us everything we need' (2 Peter 1:3).

Be-attitudes

These 'be-attitudes' or attitudes-to-be derive their name from the Latin word *beati*, meaning 'Blessed – happy, to be envied, and spiritually prosperous' (Matthew 5:3 Amplified Bible). They are more than a means of happiness; they are the source of true spiritual joy and prosperity.

Happiness is dependent on happenings. The word 'happy' comes from an old English word, hap, meaning chance. It speaks of something that comes about by chance. The term 'blessed', on the other hand, comes from the Greek word *makarios* and carries with it the idea of a joy complete in itself – a joy resistant to pain, sorrow, suffering, loss and grief. It is God's 'inexpressible and glorious joy' (1 Peter 1:8) that 'no one will take away' (John 16:22), a joy not dependent on external circumstances.

The Beatitudes challenge every aspect of human behaviour. They represent a Christian counter-culture. They are more than mere happy attitudes. They highlight the angle of approach to life that characterises a person who is truly blessed, happy and to be envied.

Theirs is the kingdom

If in each Beatitude the primary emphasis is on the word 'blessed', the secondary emphasis is most certainly on the words 'theirs' and 'they'. The original Greek language uses the emphatic pronoun which can read 'theirs and theirs only'. This underscores the importance of each redemptive attitude. In doing this the reciprocal promise attached to each Beatitude could read: 'Blessed are the pure in heart, for they [and they only] will see God' (Matthew 5:8).

As if to hold everything else in context, Jesus begins and concludes his teaching on attitudes with the same note of promise. By his embracing all eight Beatitudes with 'theirs [and theirs only] is the kingdom' (Matthew 5:3,10), Jesus portrays kingdom[1] people as those consumed with a passion to establish God's will on earth through a Christ-like character.

'The earth is the Lord's,' declares the Psalmist, 'and everything in it, the world, and all who live in it' (Psalm 24:1). The Christian church, motivated by a biblical worldview, must prioritise the issue of kingdom and become actively involved in ousting the illegal squatter. It needs to remove Satan's governmental influence from every sphere of life into which it has infiltrated, and to reinstate the rule of God. Is this not the purpose for which 'the Son of God appeared . . . to destroy the devil's work' (1 John 3:8)?

Base camp

'When he saw the crowds, he went up on a mountainside and sat down. His disciples came to him, and he began to teach them, saying: "Blessed are the poor in spirit, for theirs is the kingdom of heaven"' (Matthew 5:1–3).

No skilled mountaineer would ever attempt a major climb without first establishing a clear line of communication and supply. To reach the summit, the mountaineer first establishes a base camp, a point of reference from which all necessary supplies can be drawn for those attempting to reach the top.

On the day of Queen Elizabeth II's coronation, when the stirring news of the conquest of Mount Everest came, few people

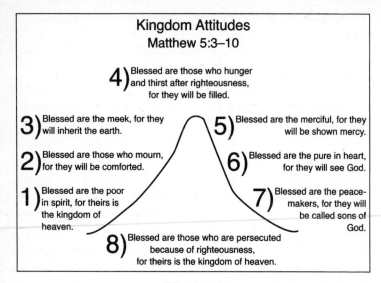

Diagram 1

realised the logistics required for such a climb. The summit reached by Sir Edmund Hillary and the Sherpa Tensing was the result of a team effort reaching back many thousands of feet. Sufficient to say that although the base camp is far removed from the summit, it is crucial to completing the challenge.

In biblical language Matthew 5:3 is a spiritual base camp to the Sermon on the Mount. 'Blessed – happy, to be envied, and spiritually prosperous . . . are the poor in spirit . . . for theirs is the kingdom of heaven!' (Amplified Bible). All that follows is supplied from this one basic attitude.

Before us lie the foothills called 'Mournful' and 'Meekness' that will ultimately lead us to the summit of divine fullness [see Diagram 1]. But 'poverty of spirit' is an attitude that, once established, will be a source of supply to every stage of our climb. Having reached the zenith of these teachings, the down-hill outworking of 'Pure in Heart', 'Making Peace' and

'Showing Mercy' will still need to be supplied from this base camp.

God's way up is down

In what is seemingly an upside-down kingdom, God's way up is down: 'Everyone who exalts himself will be humbled, and he who humbles himself will be exalted' (Luke 14:11). To become mature you must first become a child: 'Unless you change and become like little children, you will never enter the kingdom of heaven' (Matthew 18:1–6). Leadership requires the quality of servanthood, for Jesus said: 'I am among you as one who serves' (Luke 22:25–27). And to be strong a person has first to become weak. 'I delight in weaknesses,' wrote the Apostle Paul. 'For when I am weak, then I am strong' (2 Corinthians 12:10).

It is therefore not surprising that Jesus should pre-empt spiritual fullness by teaching first on the issue of emptying.

How different the school of the Holy Spirit is from the college of human experience! Humanity majors in aggression and sees self-centredness and self-sufficiency as the keys to success. This assertive approach to life treats interpersonal relationships as a means to an end and leaves both wayward children and destroyed marriages in the wake of a war that takes no prisoners.

While the university of human achievement pursues a programme of self-awareness, the school of the Spirit advocates a very different curriculum. God's way up is down. Therefore, to experience true success in life, we must first learn the lesson of 'poverty of spirit'.

The reason why some Christians have never experienced fullness is because they have never truly known emptiness. The Bible's promise of fullness is often preceded by a process of emptying. 'I will pour water on the thirsty land, and streams on the dry ground,' God says in Isaiah 44:3. The invitation of Isaiah 55:1 is to the 'thirsty'. When speaking of the outpouring of the Holy Spirit, Jesus said: 'If anyone is thirsty, let him come to me and drink' (John 7:37–39).

Thirst is the body's recognition of a vital need, a craving that becomes a singular and all-embracing pursuit of life. Rachel's thirst for children caused her to cry to God: 'Give me children, or I'll die!' (Genesis 30:1). So, too, God responds to those whose desires are centred on him.

Poverty of spirit

Some believers, comparing Matthew 5:3 with Luke 6:20, have mistakenly understood that Jesus was commending material poverty as being in itself a means of spiritual blessing. They see the lack of worldly wealth as a means of divine grace.

In his book *The Cost of Discipleship* Dietrich Bonhoeffer states: 'He calls them blessed, not because of their privation, nor the renunciation they have made, for these are not blessed in themselves. Only the call and the promise, for the sake of which they are ready to suffer poverty and renunciation, can justify the Beatitudes.' Marginal note: 'Since the days of the Clementines, Catholic exegesis has applied this Beatitude to the virtue of poverty, the *paupertas voluntaria* of the monks, or any kind of poverty undertaken voluntarily for the sake of Christ. But in both cases the error lies in looking for some kind of human behaviour as the ground for the Beatitude instead of the call and promise of Jesus alone.'[2]

The absence of prosperity and the presence of poverty as essential ingredients to extending God's kingdom on earth have in some quarters produced a mind-set and lifestyle that are both drab and depressive. Any frame of reference that refuses to accept prosperity as a means to promote the kingdom is a pro-verbial shot in the foot for the body of Christ. A mentality towards poverty that views excellence as worldly, and the inferior as acceptable, gives the church an unacceptable image in today's society.

If first impressions count, the church has to change its image so as to exemplify the excellence of God in all we do. It should be noted, though, that poverty is not to be viewed as a mark of disobedience or divine disapproval. As hunger can sharpen our desires for the natural, the absence of material wealth can increase our dependency on our heavenly Father (Luke 6:20; Matthew 6:30–34).

The day my dad purchased his first new car was a day to remember. After years of hard work and suffering the problems of cheap secondhand vehicles, he decided to buy the car of his dreams. With its shining chrome-work and its smart, white-walled tyres, this beautiful yellow-and-black 1959 Ford Consul was everything a person could ask for. Imagine my surprise, therefore, when, having driven the vehicle home and reversed it into the garage, Dad decided to leave it there for three months!

As my mentor in the area of giving, my dad taught me the importance and implications of tithes and offerings. Those who honour God, he declared, would in turn be honoured. To see his business grow, therefore, was only to be expected. But to have bought a new car and then hide it from public view was not my idea of fun.

Somehow, Dad was unable to balance the blessings of prosperity with the belief that others would see his gain as some kind of customer exploitation. Public opinion and the fear of others made it very difficult for him to enjoy the blessing of God. So there the car sat, and we had to be satisfied with an occasional sneak preview under the cover of darkness and a pretend ride in a stationary vehicle.

William Barclay, commenting on the phrase 'poor in spirit', writes: 'We must be careful not to think that this Beatitude calls actual material poverty a good thing. Poverty is not a good thing. Jesus would never have called "blessed" a state where people live in slums and have not enough to eat, and where health rots because conditions are all against it. That kind of poverty it is the aim of the Christian gospel to remove.'[3]

The poverty that Jesus is advocating here is a different kind of poverty; it is poverty of spirit: 'Blessed are the poor in spirit, for theirs is the kingdom of heaven.'

Spirit equals attitude

The Greek word *pneuma* ('spirit'), when translated as 'Spirit' with a capital 'S', normally refers to the Holy Spirit. In other cases, with a small 's', it is fluid in its use and we do well to avoid being dogmatic about its meaning.

Sometimes *pneuma* is best understood as an attitude. For example, in 1 Corinthians 4:21 we read, 'What do you prefer? Shall I come to you with a whip, or in love and with a *gentle spirit*?' In 2 Corinthians 4:13 Paul writes: '"I believed; therefore I have spoken." With that same *spirit of faith* we also believe and therefore speak.' While one translation interprets Ephesians 4:23 as, 'Be renewed in the *spirit of your mind*' (NASB), the New International Version translates it as, 'Be made new in the *attitude of your minds*.'

Paul in writing to the Thessalonians speaks of humankind as 'spirit, soul and body' (1 Thessalonians 5:23). The spirit of a person is that inner part of his being that relates to God. For instance, worship issues from the spirit of a person: 'God is spirit, and his worshippers must worship in spirit and in truth' (John 4:24). Men and women relate to God from their spirit, and vice versa: 'The Spirit himself testifies with our spirit that we are God's children' (Romans 8:16). God begins at the centre, and works out to the circumference, whereas generally we are more concerned with externals.

Humanism says: 'Improve the environment and you will

eventually improve the person.' But according to the Word of God, our problem is fundamentally one of the heart. It is in the innermost part of our being that Christ's teaching on attitude begins. Here is where the battle over behaviour is won or lost.

True poverty

The New Testament uses two words to describe poverty. The first is the noun *penes*, a Greek word used to describe a labourer who works hard to live, one who is barely existing from day to day. To miss a day's work is to miss a day's meals.

The second word is the adjective *ptochos*, the verb of which means 'to be poor as a beggar, to be destitute'. It is the desperate case of 'beg or starve'. This is used by Luke: 'At his gate was laid a beggar named Lazarus, covered with sores and longing to eat what fell from the rich man's table' (Luke 16:20–21).

It is not *penes* that is used in this Beatitude; it is *ptochos*, which describes absolute and abject poverty.

He who is 'poor in spirit' has recognised his spiritual destitution and realises he hasn't the means or ability to make up the deficiency. It is an attitude of total dependence on another to meet the supply. It is an angle of approach to life in which we have surrendered completely our independence and become totally dependent on God as our source of supply. This then is the first and foremost attitude taught by Jesus in his Sermon on the Mount. As such it is paramount in both our entry into and our continual enjoyment of the lifestyle of God's kingdom.

Dependent and interdependent

We live in a world that is suffering the effects of the 'me generation'. Our age not only undermines traditional values, but also dismisses as irrelevant the absolute truths of God's Word. It is all 'me, my and mine' as humanity ties itself up more tightly into a self-centred knot.

Such a philosophy has no place in God's kingdom, for the very nature of sin is selfishness. The self-centred nature of Satan's kingdom must not be allowed to extend its behavioural influence to the church. A spiritual environment – where leaders are more into maintenance mode than missions, pandering to the cries of 'Teach me, bless me, help me, heal me, visit me, strengthen me, encourage me and prosper me' – will detract from the eternal destiny of the church.

The self-centred, self-sufficient philosophy of humanism believes that God is irrelevant to the survival and fulfilment of the human race. This philosophy of self-exaltation also stands in direct opposition to God's government. Yet when humanity rejects God as King, we end up in the situation described in the book of Judges: 'In those days Israel had no king; everyone did as he saw fit' (Judges 21:25). It is the kind of thinking that treats God as a spare tyre, not denying his existence but consigning him to the sidelines for emergency use only. Such a value system is not kingdom thinking.

At the heart of the working relationship between God the Father, Son and Holy Spirit we find interdependence rather than independence. Jesus repeatedly pointed out that his power and authority were rooted in a healthy dependence on his Father (John 14:9–17; 5:19, 30; 8:26). Without grasping for position and recognition, Jesus emptied himself, took on the role of a servant, laid down his life and became totally obedient to his Father's will (see Diagram 2).

This is true poverty of spirit. It is also the redemptive attitude that should be ours, for 'your attitude should be the same as that of Christ Jesus' (Philippians 2:5) who 'for your sakes . . . became poor, so that you through his poverty might become rich' (2 Corinthians 8:9). This is a mind-set in which the individual has surrendered his independent approach to life and

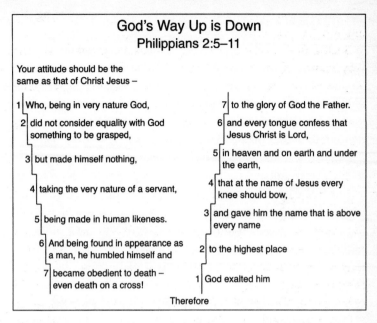

Diagram 2

become totally dependent on God for his supply. Such a person is also rightly dependent on others within the body of Christ.

The early church used this angle of approach of total dependence on God and interdependence with each other to great effect. Interpersonal relationships within the church were based not merely on corporate activities but on a commitment to care for each other. 'All the believers were one in heart and mind. No one claimed that any of his possessions was his own, but they shared everything they had' (Acts 4:32).

God is our source of supply. When we are poor in spirit we recognise not only our own deficiency but also that God and his people are our sufficiency (Philippians 4:13; Romans 8:37). With the Psalmist we declare of our God: 'All my springs of joy are in you' (Psalm 87:7 NASB).

Nature teaches us

When we look at nature we can see the economy of God in all things. 'Men are without excuse,' said the Apostle Paul, 'because God is evident in creation' (Romans 1:20 paraphrased). To the Corinthian church Paul writes: 'Does not nature itself teach' (1 Corinthians 11:14 NASB) 'first . . . the natural; then the spiritual?' (1 Corinthians 15:46 NASB).

Nature teaches us the principle that nothing is an end in itself. The problem with human philosophy is that it promotes an ideology that things, including people themselves, are an end in themselves. Yet everything has an inbuilt twofold code of self-identification and corporate integration. For instance, a human cell knows its individual function while at the same time recognising its need of others so as to make the whole. How does a kidney cell know it's not a heart cell? It's a mystery. Each cell knows its identity, yet it does not become independent. Rather, it arranges itself in the body for the benefit of the whole. 'Within each [cell] is "a rugged individuality which can go on a rampage and break laws" – as cancer cells do.'[4]

Quartzes, electrons, neutrons, molecules and galaxies all function with this twofold code. Recognising their individual uniqueness and identity, they still fit into God's larger economy. A note separated out from a musical scale becomes a dreary monotone. A typed character divorced from a word becomes a meaningless symbol. If a colour deserts its spectrum it loses its beauty. If a star forsakes its orbit it destroys itself.

God has made humankind complete while at the same time unable to function without others – interdependent rather than independent. As members of the body of Christ we must never allow our personal uniqueness, our individuality, to be submerged into a bland form of Christianity. Unity does not mean uniformity, but rather conformity to the image of Christ. While we still maintain our individual identity, we must look for our personal fulfilment in the larger setting.

People are not an end in themselves, for God has 'set eternity in their hearts' (Ecclesiastes 3:11 NASB), and therefore we must always be looking for the larger setting. That is our place, our setting in the body of Christ.

I did it my way

Personal insecurity breeds independence and if left unattended can create an intense desire for isolation. Frank Sinatra's famous melody, *I Did It My Way*, could be the theme song of those who display this negative version of 'poverty of spirit' – an independent attitude.

God has not called Christians and Christianity into isolationism: 'God setteth the solitary in families' (Psalm 68:6 KJV). Collectively, he has destined us to be 'the salt of the earth', 'the light of the world', 'a city on a hill [that] cannot be hidden' and 'the joy of the whole earth' (Matthew 5:13–14; Psalm 48:2).

The spiritual Lone Ranger, who drifts in and out of local church life, is answerable to no one and refuses to engage in any long-term commitment. Such an individual often finds personal discipleship difficult and will display some if not all of the following marks of an unteachable person:

- Values his or her own opinion – turns God's Word into his/her own ideas.
- Counters the need for change with a display of personal ability.
- Gives a display of hurt feelings.
- Pulls apart advice given.
- Is argumentative.
- Raises other issues to cloud the real problem.
- Feels he or she is a special case.

- Is stubborn.
- Sees own importance above the needs of others.
- Feels got at and hard done by.
- Is always looking for an alternative explanation to the one given.
- Only submits when routed on every argument.

Called to conquer

Now that we have established this most fundamental of kingdom attitudes, we can move forward and begin to exercise authority over what is legally and redemptively ours through the finished work of Jesus Christ.

According to this Beatitude, when we are poor in spirit, 'ours is the kingdom'. To the natural mind 'poverty of spirit' and 'inheriting the kingdom' may seem poles apart. Yet they are two sides of the same coin. When living under God's authority as his dependants, we are able to exercise authority (Luke 7:2–10).

Christians are called not to be passive spectators to life but rather to be actively involved. While some watch or wait for things to happen, those who display the winning edge make things happen. They are poor in spirit but forceful in faith. They are kingdom people who exert heaven's rule on the earth through the power and authority of the Holy Spirit.

This requires us to have the redemptive attitude of Joshua and Caleb (Numbers 14:5–8, 24). We must be willing to settle for nothing less than our full inheritance in the area of health, finances, work, home and family. We are called to conquer circumstances, not merely cope with them. When faced with any situation calculated to rob us, this attitude causes us to stand up boldly and by 'the abundance of grace and . . . the gift of righteousness . . . reign in life through the One, Jesus Christ' (Romans 5:17 NASB).

At the age of forty, Moses was a man educated in all the

wisdom of the Egyptians and powerful in speech and action. Yet he lacked a 'poverty of spirit'. As a result he used the forceful-ness of human aggression and assertiveness. Having murdered an Egyptian, he 'thought that his own people would realise that God was using him to rescue them, but they did not' (Acts 7:22–25). So he fled in fear and became an exile in Midian for forty years.

How different the man who later approached the burning bush on Mount Horeb! The experience of living in the desert had by then created in him a very different 'angle of approach'. This one-time Lone Ranger was now totally dependent on God and interdependent with others; he humbly inquired of God: 'Who am I, that I should go to Pharaoh and bring the Israelites out of Egypt?' (Exodus 3:11).

But the man who was now 'poor in spirit' was about to become 'forceful in faith'. Laying down his shepherd's staff, which in turn became a serpent, Moses initially 'fled from it', as he had run from a crisis forty years earlier. But God com-manded him to 'grasp it by its tail' (Exodus 4:4 NASB). Taking control of the situation in such a way demanded faith in God's Word. Yet Moses' obedience turned a shepherd's staff into a sceptre, an object of rule with which he would extend God's purposes on earth. In the same way, those who know a poverty of spirit can expect the fulfilment of the promise: 'Theirs is the kingdom.'

Caught in a sudden and violent storm, a man searched desper-ately for a place to shelter. He realised his own inability to cope with the wintry elements and quickly found an opening in a huge rock. Climbing into the cleft in the rock he was able to escape from the howling wind and the driving rain.

In the safety of his new-found shelter he began to think of a spiritual parallel to this experience. Possessing nothing to protect or preserve him from the storm, he had found shelter and security in the rock. The stone had become his sufficiency, making up for his own insufficiency. He reached for a scrap piece of paper and began to write:

> *'Nothing in my hand I bring*
> *Simply to the Cross I cling . . .*
> *Foul, I to the fountain fly;*
> *Wash me, Saviour, or I die.'*

In the words of this well-known hymn, A M Toplady had discovered an eternal secret. The hymn beautifully describes the attitude by which we must enter into the kingdom of God. It is an angle of approach that is as fundamental to kingdom life as a base camp 'poverty of spirit' becomes a means of grace as we continue to pursue our God-given destiny.

Notes

[1] The biblical term 'kingdom' has more to do with rule than it has with realm or territory. For instance, Jesus defined the kingdom as 'a certain nobleman [who] went to a distant country to receive a kingdom for himself, and then return' (Luke 19:12 NASB). The man didn't return with a piece of real estate tucked under his arm, but rather with authority, the 'right to rule', or as one translation puts it, 'kingly power' (RSV).

[2] Dietrich Bonhoeffer, *The Cost of Discipleship* (SCM Press, 1964).

[3] William Barclay, *The Daily Study Bible* (St Andrew's Press, 1976).

[4] Ron Trudinger, *Cells for Life* (Kingsway Publications, 1983).

REDEMPTIVE ATTITUDE No 1

'Blessed are the poor in spirit,
for theirs is the kingdom of God.'

'A non-selfish approach to life
whereby we acknowledge the need for
others and, constantly depending on God for
our source of supply, we aggressively
lay claim to all that is redemptively
ours in Christ.'

CHAPTER FOUR

GOOD GRIEF

*'Be made new in the attitude of your minds; and
. . . put on the new self, created to be like God in
true righteousness and holiness.'*

Ephesians 4:23–24

According to the conference programme, the morning had been given over to prayer. It was exciting thinking of so many church leaders calling to God on behalf of a nation.

Before we began, it was agreed to allow a young man to address the conference. As he started to speak it was obvious that he was clearly moved by the Holy Spirit. With a voice broken by the gravity of what God had shown him, he described a picture of the church. He painted with broad brush strokes the church as being malformed and immature, having a childlike body and an adult head. He struggled to compose himself as tears streamed down his face. He asked the delegates to call to God on behalf of the church, to pray that spiritual growth would cause the body of Christ to grow up.

His words pierced through the façade of religious formalism and cancelled our preconceived ideas. Cut to the quick, grown men began to fall to the ground in tears, calling on God. People started to pray earnestly. Soon the tears turned to loud crying, wailing and deep groaning. The atmosphere was electric. The united cry intensified with every passing minute, as wave after wave of godly sorrow swept through the hall.

Morning of mourning

The morning of prayer had become the prayer of mourning! Having been brought up in Pentecostal meetings, I had experienced noise and emotion, but never anything like this. In all my years of meeting and praying with Holy Spirit-filled leaders, this was a totally new experience. We had tapped into the heart of the Father and, for one brief moment, we were sharing his grief.

Still enveloped in this godly environment, I found myself asking fundamental questions: 'What is all this?' 'What's happening here?'

Immediately the Holy Spirit quickened an answer within me: 'This is mourning!'

We had become grieved with what grieves the heart of God, broken with what breaks God's heart. I was now experiencing that mourning for which Jesus congratulated his followers: 'Blessed are those who mourn' (Matthew 5:4).

Of all the eight attitudes described in the Sermon on the Mount, 'Blessed are those who mourn' has perhaps caused me more difficulty than any other.

How could Jesus consider someone 'enviably happy' (Amplified Bible) who was experiencing the trauma of bereavement? Or how could he congratulate a person suffering the loss of a loved one? But that is exactly what he seemed to be saying to the crowd on the mountainside.

Though I was happy to use the verse as sermon material for the occasional funeral, the idea of finding true joy through sorrow was somewhat foreign to me. How is it possible to picture a mourner as someone who is to be envied? Or to view bereavement as a joyful experience? Should we congratulate the bereaved on their sense of loss? Surely not, for Jesus would not condone such a callous act. But if the word 'mourning' means death, sorrow, anguish, tears and loss, then what Jesus is teaching must clearly be a contradiction of terms. How can a kingdom of 'righteousness, peace and joy in the Holy Spirit' (Romans 14:17) propound a philosophy of joyful sorrow?

It's a knockout

No wonder the crowd found his teaching amazing! (Matthew 7:28). One translator actually defines that word 'amazed' as 'to be struck with a blow, as one stricken with panic and astonishment'. In a very real sense the Sermon on the Mount was a knockout with the crowd. What he taught burst their religious bubble and struck a blow to their earthly concepts of divine government.

When they compared his words with those of the religious leaders, they noted that Jesus spoke as one who had the right to speak. He declared heaven's manifesto 'with authority' (Mark 1:22–27). Jesus represented a government that 'is not a matter of talk but of power' (1 Corinthians 4:20), a counter-culture that challenged every aspect of human behaviour.

His words of spirit and life (John 6:63,68) struck those bystanders with fear and awe. They were pole-axed by the demands of this new, incoming government. With each declaration Jesus created a shockwave that shattered the religious mind-set of his audience. He was determined to break through the defences of personal prejudice to spell out the cost of his kingdom. These were requirements like no other – and none more so than the demands of 'Blessed are those who mourn.'

In the wake of these five words the illusion that this was a governing power just like any other was finally dismissed. You can almost hear the crowd gasp in amazement, as Jesus said, 'O the perfect joy that accompanies those who are appalled by their sense of loss!'

Heading for the top

Although we are still motivated to get to the top (see Diagram 1), the reality of what is involved in the climb is beginning to dawn on us. When someone asked George Leigh Mallory if his proposed climb up Mount Everest was too dangerous for a man with a wife and children to support, his reply was, 'Yes, it's dangerous going up Mount Everest. But the greatest danger in life is not taking the adventure.'

We press upwards, still believing that from the vantage point of 'hungering and thirsting for righteousness' we will radically change our whole approach to a world in need. Yet this concept of mourning is a challenge. Maybe we ought to take another route or miss out this section of the mountain altogether? But that's not possible. There is a logical sequence to all these attitudes. Each is part of a progressive revelation. Neither haphazard nor unrelated, their order is systematic and sequential.

In order to understand mourning, it is first necessary to experience poverty of spirit. Poverty of spirit, mourning and meekness are a sequence of events, a process which in turn creates a spiritual appetite to hunger and thirst for righteousness. Reaching the top and enjoying a whole new perspective on life means travelling on a set route.

We cannot mourn before we are poor in spirit. Neither can we know real spiritual thirst until we have a working knowledge of meekness. In this way God has placed emphasis on our relationship with him before others. We cannot hope to relate correctly to other people without first being right with God.

We must first set up our base camp of total dependence on God and interdependence on his people. From here we will have to draw sufficient supplies for the whole of life's expedition. Once we have the base camp established, we can move on to redemptive attitude number two. It is the one which, in terms of the Kingdom Constitution, may be called, 'The Law of Brokenness'. As such, it is an approach to life that can be understood only by those who, like the Corinthian believers, 'have the mind of Christ' (1 Corinthians 2:16).

Eastern mourning

From an Eastern perspective, the effect of what Jesus announced would have been catastrophic. In the Western world, death and mourning are a relatively quiet, private affair. Not so in Eastern culture. Mourning was, and still is, a visible and very expressive experience, something in which the whole neighbourhood shares. It involves loud weeping, wailing and deep groaning.

When the prophet Micah warns of the imminent judgement against Samaria and Jerusalem, he describes his sorrow in these terms: 'Because of this I will weep and wail; I will go about barefoot and naked. I will howl like a jackal and moan like an owl' (Micah 1:8). Some translators interpret the word 'owl' as 'ostriches', a Hebrew word that can be rendered, 'the daughter of loud moaning or screeching'.

The Egyptian nation mourned the death of its firstborn with a loud and bitter cry (Exodus 12:30). The word used here means 'to call out for help under great distress'.[1] It is a cry of anguish (2 Kings 2:12); the cry of a woman whose body is being violated through rape (Deuteronomy 22:23–27); a cry of desperation to God for help to lead his people (Exodus 17:4); the response of Esau to the loss of his blessing and the nation of Israel's loss of the Ark of the Covenant (Genesis 27:34; 1 Samuel 4:14); the cry of those plundered and ravaged in war (Jeremiah 49:21); a loud lament of the righteous over the loss suffered by a nation (Isaiah 33:7; Lamentations 2:18).

More than anything else, it is the kind of cry that causes a heart response from God. It was those very cries of the captives of Israel in Egypt that caused God to send Moses as a deliverer (Exodus 3:7–10).

Mourning wasn't only an emotional, external process. Inner turmoil of spirit was invariably accompanied in the Old Testament by external, visible signs of that grief. Eastern mourners often wore sackcloth or dirty garments, the kind of clothes calculated to cause the most irritation and personal discomfort. By doing so, they tried to empathise with the situation or circumstance for which they were mourning. When he heard the news of Joseph's supposed death, 'Jacob tore his clothes, put on sackcloth and mourned for his son many days' (Genesis 37:34). Sackcloth not only caused discomfort; it was also a sign of sadness and mortification (Matthew 11:21).

The practice of sprinkling ashes or dust on the head was similar. While some writers see ashes as a sign of humanity's worthlessness and insignificance, others see them as a sign of humiliation used to heighten further the degree of devastation felt by the bereaved. Throwing ash into the air and allowing it to fall on the head was part of the funeral ritual (see Joshua 7:6). Some would even sit among the ashes, which was more often than not the local rubbish dump (Job 2:8).

Mourners and family members would not wash, eat or anoint themselves with oil for the time considered to be a period of mourning. As part of the sorrow King David suffered for his shameful act of adultery with Bathsheba, he neither 'washed, put on lotions [nor] changed his clothes' (see 2 Samuel 12:20).

Sometimes mourners would shave off their hair. They did this to remove what might cause them personal pride, pleasure or protection from the sun's heat. We catch a glimpse of this concerning the absence of mourners for Israel: 'No one will cut himself or shave his head for them. No one will offer food to comfort those who mourn . . . nor will anyone give them drink to console them' (Jeremiah 16:6–7). Although mutilation of the body was strictly forbidden (Leviticus 19:28; Deuteronomy 14:1), cutting off the beard wasn't (Isaiah 15:2).

Is it therefore any wonder that the reaction of the crowd, on hearing Jesus speak of the blessedness of mourning, was one of amazement? The concept of a joyful mourner was indeed a strange one.

Utter devastation

In the minds of those who listened to Jesus, mourning was not some quiet, joyful affair, but rather a verbal, visible demonstration of *being utterly devastated*.

It is this frame of reference that helps us to understand where Jesus was coming from in his teaching on this second redemptive attitude. Remember, Jesus was not referring to the sorrow and mourning that accompanies natural death. As with all the other Beatitudes, the issue is a spiritual one. When he spoke of poverty and hunger, he was dealing with spiritual poverty and spiritual hunger. The kingdom of God comes to answer the cry of poverty and hunger, not to condone it.

What we have before us is therefore a graphic description of spiritual brokenness, or what I would prefer to call spiritual sensitivity. This is an attitude in which we are sensitive to, and devastated by, the loss that we ourselves or others may be suffering. It is having the heart of God on an issue, seeing something as a clear violation of the revealed will of God.

As we are moved by the Holy Spirit's interaction with our spirit we become deeply moved to do whatever is necessary to see the situation resolved. In so doing, as a mourner, I am empathising with the loss. My whole being is taken up with it. Food and sleep become unimportant. Whatever it takes to resolve this issue in itself becomes food and drink to the mourner. Kittel describes the meaning behind this phrase 'to mourn' as, 'Passionate grief which leads to corresponding action'.[2]

When we view Jesus' words in the light of an Eastern mind-set we can begin to understand this second kingdom attitude. To mourn means to be sensitive, inwardly broken and utterly devastated by the sense of loss. It is a unique move of the Holy Spirit in which God's people become overawed by what they see; as such it should never become a formal response to a crisis. In New Testament times, some people had become so professional in the art of mourning that their expertise was hired to assist a family in times of grief. It was professionals like these whom Jesus dismissed at the funeral of Jairus's daughter (Mark 5:38–40).

Jesus had not come to further such institutionalised patterns of behaviour, but to express emotions with their source in the heart of his Father. What, then, of mourning today? How is such a sense of utter devastation portrayed in a Christian's angle of approach to people, objects and events now?

Good mourning

In the Sermon on the Mount Jesus is not referring to 'worldly sorrow', whose only result is 'death'. Nor is he speaking of a simple stirring of the emotions – though that is involved (Matthew 27:3–4; Hebrews 12:16–17). Rather, he is talking about a 'godly sorrow [that] brings deliverance' (2 Corinthians 7:8–11). According to Paul's letter to the church at Corinth this contains four major ingredients:

• Eagerness to see the wrong corrected.
• Indignation at a violation of God's revealed will.
• Zeal to do God's will.
• Readiness to do whatever is necessary to put things right.

To mourn, therefore, is to experience an inner action of God's Spirit with our spirit in which we see and sense a situation from God's viewpoint. Once we recognise a matter to be a violation of God's revealed will, we become so deeply affected by what we see with our mind's eye that everything becomes expendable in the interests of change. Utterly devastated, we are ready, if necessary, to suffer personal inconvenience in order to bring divine order. Such feelings of utter devastation drive us to deal radically with ourselves and others.

Such grief motivates us to intercede on behalf of others, sometimes with tears, 'groans that words cannot express' (Romans 8:26), lamenting and wailing. This angle of approach or attitude is not only fundamental to our new birth but also plays a key role in our ongoing kingdom lifestyle.

True mourning breaks the boundaries of our self-imposed comfort zone. It changes not only our thinking but our lifestyle. This beautiful attitude will motivate us to maintain a redemptive rather than an adversarial approach to people and events.

We are not talking here about an emotional ego trip. Rather, inner brokenness arises from the indwelling nature of Christ. It causes us to feel the pain of those who have been hurt, offended and abused.

Mourning adjusts our world view. Mourners are no longer able to watch the media's portrayal of a tragic world event without being motivated to respond. Whether offering practical help or giving themselves to intercessory prayer, mourners who are to be congratulated grieve for the hurting, abused and offended and sacrificially work towards change.

The principle is the same in the arena of international conflict and the crucible of interpersonal relationships. Mourning is a physical action, not a mental assent. Any breakdown in communication or rift between two parties generates within mourners a deep sense of loss. They make themselves vulnerable as they lay down their lives to work towards reconciliation.

Be they offended or offender, true mourners are stirred to act in a redemptive manner. Celebrational mourning is a be-attitude – an attitude to be.

The law of brokenness

In the preface to his *Studies in Sermon on the Mount*, Dr Martyn Lloyd-Jones writes: 'If you read the history of the church you will find it has always been when men and women have taken this sermon seriously, and faced themselves in the light of it, that true revival has come.'[3]

Godly grief has always been a hallmark of true revival. Quoting Charles Finney, Oswald Smith wrote in his book *The Revival We Need*: 'It loaded me down with agony. As I returned to my room I felt almost as if I should stagger under the burden that was on my mind; and I struggled, and groaned and agonised, but could not frame to present the case before God in words, but only in groans and tears. The Spirit struggled within me with groanings that could not be uttered.'

David Brainerd recalled a similar experience: 'Near the middle of the afternoon God enabled me to wrestle ardently in intercession for my friends. But just at night the Lord visited me marvellously in prayer. I think my soul never was in such an agony before. I felt no restraint; for my friends, for the ingathering of souls, for multitudes of poor souls and for many whom I thought were the children of God, personally in many different places. I was in such agony from sun up, half an hour high, till near dark, that I was all over wet with sweat.'

One person wrote of the Welsh revival: 'Such real travail of soul for the unsaved I have never before witnessed. I have seen young Evan Roberts convulsed with grief, and calling on his audience to pray.' Another added, 'It was not the eloquence of Evan Roberts that broke men down, but his tears. He would break down, crying bitterly for God to bend them, in an agony of prayer, the tears coursing down his cheeks, with his whole frame writhing. Strong men would break down and cry like children. Women would shriek. A sound of weeping and wailing would fill the air. Evan Roberts in the intensity of his agony would fall in the pulpit, while many in the crowd often fainted.'[4]

Just as harvest is the fulfilment of a process initiated by the farmer's plough breaking up the fallow ground, so brokenness in God's economy always proceeds blessedness. Before the builder can erect a house he will invariably have to pull down or dig up whatever might hinder the establishing of something new.

The 'broken and contrite heart, O God, you will not despise' (Psalms 51:17). As the jar of expensive perfume expressed the broken selfless abandonment of the women who anointed Jesus, so God exalts the humble. The selfless individual who pours out his life as to the Lord in sacrificial service becomes 'a fragrant offering, an acceptable sacrifice, pleasing to God' (Philippians 4:18).

In both the Old and New Testaments God seemingly specialises in taking the broken to demonstrate his eternal purpose. We read of broken vessels (Judges 7:19–20); a broken axe (2 Kings 6:1–6); a broken bone (Judges 15:14–17; 2 Kings 13:21); broken ground (Hosea 10:12); a broken bottle (Mark 14:3); and broken bread (Matthew 26:26). In this use of the broken, God illustrates his desire to use 'the foolish things of the world to shame the wise; God chose the weak things of the world to shame the strong. He chose the lowly things . . . the despised things . . . the things that are not – to nullify the things that are, so that no one may boast before him' (1 Corinthians 1:27–29).

Many of God's servants carry the scars of past battles, the marks of a skirmish, the bruises of an encounter. Yet to walk with a Jacob-type limp is the mark of a broken vessel fit for the Master's use.

Stinkin' thinkin'

In a world hardened by the violence and horrors of social deprivation, it is easy to become callous and untouched by the catalogue of human tragedies that surround us. As citizens of God's kingdom, though, we are called to maintain an attitude of spiritual sensitivity – to sense the Holy Spirit's prompting and be grieved by what grieves the heart of God. We are to avoid the attitude of those referred to who have become 'separated from the life of God because of the ignorance that is in them due to the hardening of their hearts. Having lost all sensitivity, they have given themselves over to sensuality' (Ephesians 4:18–19).

It is symptomatic of the age we live in to be unmoved by what moves the heart of God. While some people may choose to cross the road to avoid humanity in need, the issues of cardboard cities, single parenthood, AIDS, poverty, homelessness and drug addiction have to be faced. Is it that the church has to get down off her high horse, regain her spiritual sensitivity and begin to pour in the oil of social justice and the wine of practical care?

What was it that made William Wilberforce work so hard for the abolition of slavery? Why did Lord Shaftesbury challenge the appalling conditions imposed by greedy managers on child labour in England? What caused Oliver Cromwell to stand against the demands of an earthly king or David Brainerd to turn his back on wealth to spread the gospel? It was a spiritual sensitivity to the plight of their fellow-men and -women. Moved by the prevailing conditions of their day, they refused to distance themselves from contemporary social evils. These reformers, as salt and light in the earth, rejected a Christian ghetto mentality and chose instead to practise a gospel that was good news to the poor, freedom for prisoners, sight for the blind and release for the oppressed.

'God has a university. It's a small school. Few enrol, even fewer graduate. Very, very few indeed. God has this school because he does not have broken men. Instead he has several other types of men. He has men who claim to be God's authority . . . and aren't; men who claim to be broken . . . and aren't. And men who are God's authority, but who are unbroken. And he has, regretfully, a spectroscopic mixture of everything in-between. All of these he has in abundance; but broken men, hardly at all.'[5]

Hardening of the attitudes

In his book *See You at the Top* the author Zig Ziglar speaks of the need to avoid at all cost the deadliest of all diseases – hardening of the attitudes: 'It affects people of all ages and crosses all race, creed and colour lines. It causes more physical and emotional problems than all other diseases combined. It sends more people to an early grave, breaks up more marriages, orphans more children, causes more unemployment, sends more people to the welfare rolls, creates more drug addicts and alcoholics and causes more crime than all other diseases combined. Additionally, it is the most contagious disease known to man. The dread disease is "hardening of the attitudes" and it's caused by "stinkin' thinkin".'[6]

In biblical terminology this dreadful disease is 'the hardening of the heart', where 'heart' is used to describe the very centre of one's inner life. The heart is the fulcrum of all feeling, the seat of all emotions, desires and passions. It is the source of all thought and reflection, the seat of the will, the source of our resolve. Harbour a wrong attitude here and it is going to affect your whole life. Once the heart becomes callous, insensitive, harsh and exacting, our whole life will produce such fruits, affecting those we come into contact with. It is a condition symptomatic of someone who has become callous, unyielding, stubborn, thick skinned, hard, insensitive, unreceptive and lacking in sensitivity. The New Testament word used to describe this condition is the noun *poroun* and the verb *porosis*. Medically, the Greeks used the basic stem of this word to describe the chalk stone that forms in the human joints causing paralysis. The word was also used when speaking of a callus formed on a person's hand through digging or other similar activities. The word later became used when describing the 'loss of sensitivity or feeling', in other words, hardened skin that could not be penetrated by a needle. Later still, the Greek word took on the meaning of 'an inability to see'.

From this we can deduce that a hard-hearted man was, in New Testament terms, someone who had become insensitive and was unable to perceive spiritual things.

Mourning for what?

Such heartfelt grief, advocated by Jesus as a redemptive attitude, could be for yourself, others or even a nation. Hannah mourned for a 'son' (1 Samuel 1:10,15–17,20). Ezra grieved over the 'unfaithfulness' of God's people (Ezra 10:6). Nehemiah mourned for a 'city' (Nehemiah 1:1–10). Daniel mourned for 'understanding' (Daniel 10:1–10). Jesus demonstrated the mourner's angle of approach to life when, deeply moved and full of compassion, he wept over Jerusalem (Luke 19:41).

Jesus felt compassion for those people who were distressed and downcast (Matthew 9:36), people not attaining their rightful destiny in life (Matthew 15:32). The Apostle Paul grieved bitterly for those of his own nation who were as yet unregenerate (Romans 9:2–5). He also mourned for the church at Galatia, for they had begun well, but were now trying to attain their goal by human effort alone (Galatians 3:1–3).

Grief is an emotion felt by the person of the Holy Spirit. It is being grieved with what grieves the Holy Spirit of God. Grieving is an emotion of the Holy Spirit; Ephesians 4:30 speaks of our 'not grieving the Holy Spirit'. The Greek word translated here as 'grieve' means 'to wound', 'to cause pain, distress or suffering'. The Holy Spirit is personally offended and grieved by what he sees as a violation of God's will. Those who mourn tap into the heart of God and experience that same sorrow.

Lord Jesus, help us to remain spiritually sensitive so that we grieve for what is grieving you. Change our callous hearts and soften the resilience we have built up through the years.

Promised comfort

Each Beatitude has a clear reciprocal promise interwoven into its declared intent. For instance, the 'poor in spirit' attain the kingdom, the 'meek' inherit the earth, and so on. The promise accompanying this Beatitude is: 'for they shall be comforted'. Jesus assured his disciples that the coming Holy Spirit would be their 'Comforter' or 'Counsellor', literally, 'one called along-side to help' (John 14:16, 26).

Some people try to find a solace in ways other than mourn-ing. They seek to forget, ignore or excuse their spiritual crisis. Instead of mourning the loss, they choose to comfort them-selves with such statements as: 'I couldn't help it.' 'I've done nothing wrong.' 'Everybody does it.' 'It wasn't my fault.' This can never substitute for the work of the Comforter.

Others try desperately to justify their rebellious actions, pre-ferring to give sophisticated names to sin. It's a bit like the little girl who asked: 'Mummy, why is it that when you get irritable you call it nerves; when I get irritable you say it's temper?' In the same way, lust becomes admiration, offence becomes hurt and lies are known as exaggeration. This form of self-justifica-tion is a cover-up that will never bring true peace and joy.

The upper room gives us a biblical scenario of true and false comfort. Jesus warned his disciples that 'one of you is a devil' and that 'one of you will betray me' (John 6:66–71). He was referring to Judas and Peter, both of whom were warned of what was pending. When they had both committed their awful deeds, each sought to find his own comfort. Judas returned to the priests for solace. Unable to find peace, he hanged himself (Matthew 27:1–5). He opted out, taking the way of ultimate self-comfort. Peter, on the other hand, was utterly devastated and appalled by what he had done. He 'wept bitterly' (Luke 22:61–62). Jesus rewarded him in making a special request that he be told the good news of the resurrection: 'Go, tell my disciples and Peter' (Mark 16:7).

'Blessed are those who mourn, for they will be comforted.' Whereas one man turned to religion and found nothing but emptiness, the other turned to God and through true repentance found true comfort.

When my first form of ministerial transport wouldn't start in the mornings, as was often the case, a kind member of the church would bring his new car alongside mine and link our batteries by means of a set of starter-leads. My powerless battery would then draw from his charged one. In this way, the sufficiency of one made up the deficiency in the other.

That is just how things work in the realm of the person and power of the Holy Spirit. As we mourn the loss of our standing before a righteous God, we not only acknowledge our deficiency, but also recognise our need of one who is all-sufficient. The Holy Spirit reciprocates by drawing alongside to help.

This principle is clearly characterised in the words of James: '"God opposes the proud but gives grace to the humble." Submit yourselves, then, to God. Resist the devil, and he will flee from you. Come near to God and he will come near to you. Wash your hands, you sinners, and purify your hearts, you double-minded. Grieve, mourn and wail. Change your laughter to mourning and your joy to gloom. Humble yourselves before the Lord, and he will lift you up' (James 4:6–10).

The same promise can also be seen in Paul's writings to a church in crisis at Corinth. He begins his second letter by referring to the 'God of all comfort', speaking first of the grief caused by sexual immorality in the church. Having recognised the penitent brother, he calls for forgiveness and comfort (2 Corinthians 1:3; 2:1–8). 'Those who sow in tears will reap with songs of joy' (Psalm 126:5).

The prophet Isaiah takes up the same theme, speaking of an anointing that comes on those who 'mourn in Zion' (Isaiah 61:2–3 NASB), so as 'to grant [consolation and joy] to those who mourn in Zion, to give them an ornament – a garland or diadem – of beauty instead of ashes, the oil of joy for mourning, the garment [expressive] of praise instead of a heavy, burdened and failing spirit' (Isaiah 61:3 Amplified Bible). Those who mourn will rise up in the power of the Holy Spirit to 'rebuild the ancient ruins', 'raise up the former desolations', 'renew the ruined cities'.

Comfort comes

It was a cold winter's morning that welcomed the funeral cortège, as it slowly picked its way through the dampened stone epitaphs that stood as constant reminders of humankind's mortality. Grief-stricken relatives watched as the coffin was lowered into the gaping hole in the ground. The silence of the graveyard was broken only by the voice of an aged cleric dutifully reading set Scriptures.

As a former serviceman, my departed cousin had been very involved in fundraising for various charities. Much time and effort had gone into building his business and aiding various worthy causes. But now his life was over, and the remains of someone who had little time for God were about to be put to rest. Bowed head and tearful farewells emphasised the sense of hopelessness of a life without God.

Family and friends looked longingly into the open grave.

'If only a cure could have been found.'

'If only we could have had more time.' But the ravages of cancer had done their worst, and death seemed so final.

Just then the silence was broken by the sound of a low-flying aircraft approaching very fast. All eyes were now upwards. Fingers began to point to the sky as a Second World War Spitfire flew low over our heads. In a mark of respect and appreciation for charitable work done by my cousin, the Royal Air Force organised this magnificent farewell salute. After flying over our heads once, the pilot returned to perform what is termed the 'victory roll'.

The whole scene had changed. Heads that were bowed now looked up, hearts that were dejected now caught a glimmer of hope. Amidst a human tragedy, a reminder of triumph and victory was being enacted before our very eyes.

Out of mourning comes the promised comfort. It isn't mere sympathy, but the powerful assistance of the indwelling Holy Spirit. With the help of the Comforter we are equipped to raise up a glorious testimony to God and his kingdom, expressed through a people who feel acutely what God feels.

Our prayer must be that of Dr Jowett: 'Let my heart be broken with the things that break the heart of God.' Help me to stay spiritually sensitive, to grieve with what grieves the Holy Spirit. Change my often callous heart, hardened after years of bitter experiences, to be always sensitive to you.

Notes

[1] Harris, Archer & Waltke, *Old Testament Word Studies* (Moody Press, 1981).

[2] Kittel & Friedrich, *Theological Dictionary of the New Testament* (Eerdmans, 1976).

[3] Martyn Lloyd-Jones, *Studies in Sermon on the Mount* (IVP, 1971).

[4] Frank Bartleman, *What Really Happened at Azusa Street?* (Bridge Publishing, 1980).

[5] Gene Edwards, *A Tale of Three Kings: A Study in Brokenness* (Christian Books Publishing House, 1980).

[6] Zig Ziglar, *See You at the Top* (Baptist Spanish Publishing House, 1982).

REDEMPTIVE ATTITUDE No 2

'Blessed are those who mourn,
for they will be comforted.'

'A spiritual sensitivity that
causes me to be appalled at
that which is a clear violation
of God's revealed will. Plus a
willingness to engage the
Holy Spirit's power to restore
what is lost.'

CHAPTER FIVE

BIT AND BRIDLE SYNDROME

'Examine me, O Lord, and test me; test my soul and my attitude.'

Psalm 26:2 [NEW BERKELEY VERSION]

Twenty metres to the right of where I stood, a crazy young man lowered himself on to the back of an enraged horse. The announcer's voice boomed out of the giant loudspeakers as he outlined the rules of the competition and introduced both cowboy and horse.

The crowd grew quiet. The cowboy, who would have to stay on the horse for eight seconds holding on with only one hand, took a deep breath and nodded.

The chute door swung open. Announcer and crowd started yelling!

The horse exploded out of the gate and immediately began to spin rapidly as it kicked its rear legs high in the air, shook its body, jerked its head from side to side and lurched this way and that across the arena.

The cowboy gripped the horse as tightly as possible. His free hand waved up and down in the air to help maintain his balance. It was danger, power, brute force, flying clods of dirt, a cavernous animal snorting, and wildly cheering fans. This was the rough-and-tumble world of the rodeo cowboy.

Rodeos, the sport of cowboys, were originally nothing more than an informal gathering of local ranchers during a cattle round-up that soon developed into an ideal opportunity for farmers to show off their riding skills. A hundred and fifty years ago most cowboys were young. Young men then, as now, were often less interested in intellectual pursuits than in who was the toughest, fastest and strongest.

Their cowboy craft required strength, courage and certain very specific skills. Calves that needed branding did not come when called. They had to be chased down and lassoed. The horses that could catch those calves did not voluntarily give up their freedom for the saddle and bridle. They had to be taught their new role in a hurry, so someone had to get a saddle on them, then hang on until they accepted their new lifestyle.

They shoot horses with broken legs, don't they?

Although the thrills and spills of the Wild West Show may be the kind of excitement awaiting visitors to North America, this kind of reactionary behaviour is not limited to wild horses. Creatures of the *Homo sapiens* variety are known to react to discipline and authority in a similar way. How many of us have known people who are a law to themselves? Independent, isolated, bad-tempered and arrogant, they buck every attempt made to get a handle on their lives.

Unless men and women learn the basic principles of self-control they will continue on the downward spiral of their own rebellious nature. Without discipline, none of us can hope to understand, let alone reach, our full potential in life. Fundamental to all social order is the need for *self-control*.

Although children may need to be disciplined to correct their rebellious behaviour, it is hoped that maturity will teach them how to control their waywardness without the need of such parental correction.

The schoolboy who neglects his homework may be detained after school until the work is completed. The hope is that in time the student will learn that self-control brings rewards of freedom of time, the absence of conflict, high marks and better prospects in future life. The ungoverned man may revert to crime. He may steal, destroy, murder or rape. The failure to control himself means that others will need to govern his behaviour through penal correction.

Self-control involves governing our motives, attitudes, desires and actions. The biblical character Reuben, one of Jacob's twelve sons, is characterised as being a man who 'boils over'. 'Reuben, you are my first-born, my might and the beginning (the first fruits) of my manly strength and vigour; [your birthright gave you] the pre-eminence in dignity and the pre-eminence in power. But unstable and boiling over like water you shall not excel and have the pre-eminence [of the firstborn], because you went to your father's bed; you defiled it; you went to my couch!' (Genesis 49:3–4 Amplified Bible).

Although he was pre-eminent in nearly every area of life except his character, Reuben lacked self-control and therefore forfeited his rights and potential as the firstborn. In the same way, Saul and Solomon lost their right to the throne because they refused to govern themselves.

Joseph, on the other hand, showed great fortitude of mind and self-control. Although he was challenged by considerable peer pressure, temptation and the possibility of personal gain, he refused to capitulate. Rather than succumb to the seductive advances of Potiphar's wife he chose to govern his natural desires and escape the temptation (Genesis 39:7–23; 49:23–24).

Results of such action are not always immediate (for example, Joseph's time in jail). But having exercised authority Joseph was given authority. Being put 'in charge of the whole land of Egypt . . . Pharaoh said to Joseph, "I am Pharaoh, but without your word no one will lift hand or foot in all Egypt"' (Genesis 41:41, 44). Having first governed himself, Joseph was judged fit to rule others.

You can be the proud owner of a world-champion racehorse or have a share in a multi-million pound syndicate Derby winner, but if your prize possession happens to break its leg it will be considered worthless. No matter how bristling with promise a person might be, a stubborn attitude renders him or her useless. By refusing to accept correction we forfeit the right to realise our full potential in God, for those who exercise authority must first experience authority.

John came to our local church, a young man full of promise. We were bereft of a musician and the congregation was in desperate need of a pianist. John was keen to evangelise and was also musically adept. He seemed to be the answer to a leader's prayer. His measure of musical ability not only included various instruments but also the writing, composing and directing of gospel musicals. He quickly established himself as a very gifted player and was invited to take on the role of chief musician, songwriter and worship leader.

But John had a problem. He was arrogant, self-willed, independent and unteachable under pressure. John portrayed the classic symptoms of a bad attitude. We recognised his unique musical gift and wanted to help him reach his full potential. We sought to work alongside him so as to address these negative elements. Yet the harder we tried to help him get a grip on his life, the more John bucked and kicked. He knew best and no one was going to tell him how to run his life!

An authoritarian father had produced a son with a warped understanding of discipline and authority. To him, rule was restrictive and inconvenient, and therefore a hindrance to his free, creative and artistic spirit. Discipline – so he thought – could never be part of God's training process towards ultimate release. If the school of the Spirit included discipleship in its syllabus, John was opting out.

His arrogant 'get off my back' attitude became apparent in the church, his marriage and his business career. He chose to spend time writing music rather than time with his wife and child. As a result, his spiritual and secular life deteriorated to an all-time low. By his making numerous career changes John's undisciplined attitude proved very expensive. This Reuben-type character, of little use to God or people, lost out on all that was potentially his.

Eventually, after numerous people tried to help him get a grip on his life and rein himself in, he decided to leave the church. He was now free to roam the wide open prairies of Christendom, stopping only to drink at various charismatic waterholes. He had joined the thousands of other Lone Rangers who exile themselves in a dusty plain of spiritual independence rather than submit to God's rule.

As stubborn as a ...

Like the proverbial mule, unregenerate people are born stubborn and self-centred. They are sired by father Adam and their rebellious character is in desperate need of a radical rebirth. The prophet Jeremiah, speaking of Israel's uncontrolled lifestyle, describes them as being like 'wild donkeys'. They show no measure of personal restraint, running wild, freely venting every natural instinct and exercising little if any rule over their wild desires (see Jeremiah 2:24–25).

Isaiah adds weight to the indictment by accrediting the ox and the donkey with a greater sense of ownership than rebellious Israel (see Isaiah 1:2–4). When describing the non-Christian, the Apostle Paul speaks of those who 'followed the ways of this world . . . disobedient . . . gratifying the cravings of our sinful nature and following its desires and thoughts' (see Ephesians 2:1–3). It is this unruly nature that has to be broken, and the bit and bridle of godly discipline applied, if we are to be of any use to the Master.

The root problem for the rebellious person is a heart issue. Jesus put it like this: 'Out of the heart come evil thoughts, murder, adultery, sexual immorality, theft, false testimony, slander' (Matthew 15:19). The human approach is to start at the circumference of people's need and work towards the centre of their nature. 'Change a person's environment and you will change the person,' I hear the humanist cry. God's way is to change the people's rebellious nature, so that they in turn will change their surroundings.

External control might bring people back on the trail for a time, but only a divine intervention in human affairs will ultimately control a society unable to control itself. The answer is new birth, or as Paul writes: 'If anyone is in Christ, he is a new creation' (2 Corinthians 5:17). By turning away from my old lifestyle and identifying myself by faith with the 'cross-work' of Christ, 'the old (previous moral and spiritual condition) has passed away. Behold, the fresh and new has come!' (2 Corinthians 5:17 Amplified Bible).

Meekness, not weakness

We have established a base camp in the area of 'poverty of spirit' and gained a foothold in the truth concerning 'spiritual sensitivity'. We can now begin our final assault towards the summit of 'divine righteousness' and its fullness. Only those who maintain the spiritual high ground are best suited to relate to the needs of today's society.

But before we can taste the delights of divine fullness we must get to grips with the biblical concepts of meekness. 'Blessed are the meek, for they will inherit the earth' (Matthew 5:5). This redemptive attitude has been translated as: 'The humble and gentle attitude which expresses itself in a patient submissiveness to offence, free from malice and desire for revenge.'[1]

For most English-speaking people, the word 'meekness' has unfortunate connotations. Meekness is often associated with weakness and effeminacy. The original word does not convey this. The Bible says: 'The man Moses was very meek, above all the men which were upon the face of the earth' (Numbers 12:3

KJV). This same Moses killed an Egyptian and was a man of action. In Moses, meekness does not equate with weakness.

William Barclay, commenting on this word 'meek', writes: 'In our modern English idiom the word "meek" is hardly one of the honourable words of life. Nowadays it carries with it an idea of spinelessness, and subservience, and mean-spiritedness. It paints the picture of a submissive and ineffective creature. But it so happens that the word meek – in Greek *praus* – was one of the great Greek ethical words.'[2]

The easy-going, don't rock the boat, play-it-safe attitude that the world sees as meekness is not the spiritual virtue advocated by Jesus. Kingdom meekness is gentle and controlled strength. It is an attitude in which we hold every natural impulse in neutral ready to respond to the Holy Spirit's prompting.

Meekness is the opposite to self-assertiveness and self-interest. It is a life submitted to the Master's reins, one whose strength of character is harnessed and focused towards establishing God's ways. As such, Christians are charged to show 'all meekness unto all men' (Titus 3:2 KJV), to 'put on therefore, as the elect of God . . . meekness' (Colossians 3:12 KJV). Meekness is not weakness, but great strength; meekness is power that is bridled and therefore full of potential.

Bit-and-bridle syndrome

As well as conveying the idea of humility, the New Testament word for 'meekness' (*prautes*) was used by Greeks to describe the process by which they domesticated animals. A young colt, for instance, although full of potential, is of no use to anyone unless broken and harnessed for service.

As it wildly careers over open ground, powerful and full of potential, the animal knows few limitations on its life. For that power to be harnessed, someone has to gain control; it is possible to exercise authority over a horse by teaching it to respond to the rein. By applying pressure to the sensitive areas of the horse's anatomy, the master teaches the horse to respond to his promptings. Only when a relationship has been established, and the colt submits, is it able to serve its master. Its strength has not been reduced but is now channelled as a result of discipline.

The attitude of meekness is the opposite to self-assertiveness. It is self-control exercised through the power of the Holy Spirit (see Galatians 5:23). Jesus is not advocating or praising a natural ability to control one's self. It is all too often beyond us, naturally speaking, to suppress our emotions, impulses and passions in a purposeful way. Jesus is commending the person who is God-controlled, who has learned to recognise and respond to the divine reins of his Word and Spirit.

As if to illustrate the importance of controlled strength, Jesus rode an untamed colt into Jerusalem. It had never been broken or bridled, yet it submitted fully to the disciples, who had themselves submitted to the command of Jesus (see Luke 19:29–35). From this incident we can learn some principles involved in how to achieve the controlled life:

- The need for a faith-response to the authority of God's Word.
- A recognition of divine and delegated authority: Jesus gave the disciples authority to untie the colt. The owner responded to the request.
- The refusal of all other claims to ownership.
- A willingness to yield all rights and submit to the lordship of Christ.

In practical terms this means:

- Being prepared to take God at his word.
- Letting go of things we stubbornly cling to.
- Refusing to be owned by anything or anyone other than Christ.
- Willingly submitting to Christ's lordship of our lives.

Those who are born of the Holy Spirit have surrendered their rights as well as given up their wrongs. In Old Testament times, the vendor would take off his sandal and give it to the purchaser to seal the sale and transfer of territory. This was a public declaration of his willingness to surrender his right to walk over the land as the one who owned it. In the same way, redemption involves an acknowledging of Jesus as Lord as well as accepting him as Saviour. We voluntarily hand over all personal rights to our lives and invite the new owner to do with us as he sees fit.

Meekness is an attitude in which we maintain a willingness and openness for God to do just that. A bridle is for restraint, control and direction; through it, the horse knows its master's will. Its use will cause an animal eventually to yield its strength and thus reach its full potential in the hands of its trainer.

God's gymnasium

We, too, are in training. When Paul told Timothy to 'train' himself to be godly (1 Timothy 4:7; 2 Timothy 2:15; 3:10–17), he used the Greek word *gymnazo*, from which derives our English word 'gymnastics'. He was literally saying, 'gymnase yourself' – sharpen and develop your life and ministry through the disciplined application of truth.

Disciples are learners. But they are more than mere students. They are people who are committed to the person doing the teaching. When John's disciples fasted, they reflected the kind of man John was. Similarly, the Pharisees reproduced followers 'twice as much a son of hell' as themselves (Matthew 23:15). And as Jesus called people to follow him, he stated the personal commitment required: 'Take my yoke upon you and learn from me' (Matthew 11:29). Discipleship is learning in the context of a yoke.

In commissioning the church, Jesus said that the essence of

making disciples is 'teaching them to obey' (Matthew 28:18–20). It involves what the Apostle Paul calls 'admonition'. This is a word not widely used or understood today. In the Colossian letter the writer differentiates between this and teaching. While the term 'teaching' can be a very general concept, 'admonition' carries the thought of continuity and training. For instance, '"though Eli remonstrated with [i.e. protested to] his sons, he failed to admonish them," that is to train them continuously with the Word of God (see 1 Samuel 2:24; 3:13).'[2]

Only a loving, nurturing and secure environment can hope to encourage changes in people's lives. The ill-treatment that life often deals out can create a void of suspicion, hesitancy, uncertainty and mistrust. It is a gulf that has to be bridged if we are to listen to the advice and counsel of others.

When taking up the role of house-parents in a new children's home, some friends of mine decided to buy a horse. After first trading in an old, bedraggled donkey, they managed to buy a fine pedigree pony. The animal went by the name of 'Fireball XL Five' and showed great promise. It looked ideal to use for riding lessons, but first the animal needed to be trained. Because of previous ill-treatment, the animal was untrained and unrideable.

After a great deal of time and effort, the weeks of hand-feeding and acts of kindness began to pay off. At last they were able to get the pony to accept a bit and bridle and then eventually a saddle. But, sadly, that was as far as the training process ever got. The patience of the staff was not shared by the children. During a spell when the house-parents were away from the home one of the children decided to speed up the training programme by using a pool cue across its flanks. As a result, the pony reverted to its old ways and never regained its trust in anyone from that home!

The Apostle Paul referred to his time with the church at Ephesus with the comment: 'Be always alert and on your guard, being mindful that for three years I never stopped night or day seriously to admonish and advise and exhort you one by one' (see Acts 20:31 Amplified Bible). That's disciplining – training in the context of a yoke!

Meekness is a redemptive attitude by which we allow the dealings of God and people into our lives without thought of retaliation or reaction. We waive our rights, convinced of God's will. Through the influence of God's Holy Spirit and the application of his truth, we decide to act with self-control, not self-assertiveness or self-interest. We allow the dealings of God to control and direct our energies into good works which in turn build the kingdom.

When he was opposed by Miriam and Aaron, Moses – a man noted for his meekness (Numbers 12:3) – did not retaliate. Instead, as is so often seen in this man's life, his approach was to allow God's dealings to control and direct things. Jesus similarly epitomised this attitude. 'When they hurled their insults at him, he did not retaliate; when he suffered, he made no threats. Instead, he entrusted himself to him who judges justly' (1 Peter 2:23).

How often, when faced with God's pull of adjustment in our lives, do we want to 'buck authority'?

Authority: Restriction or release?

We live in an age where freedom and authority are viewed as opposites. Those who advocate discipline are seen as diametrically opposed to those who express a free spirit. We have a generation subscribing to the theory that the behavioural patterns of our forefathers are archaic and therefore irrelevant. Today's generation openly challenges the chain of command that previously characterised the nuclear family. The gauntlet that is being slapped in the face of historic human values is the one of the right to rule. People cry out for equal rights, human rights, workers' rights and women's rights. All these serve to spotlight the question that faces a culture in crisis: 'Authority: Who has it and who dares to exercise it?'

Into this world theatre the church must emerge as salt and light and be at the forefront of the authority argument. If the church were to abstain through indifference, isolation or ignorance, it would, in effect, create a moral vacuum in which humanity would implode and self-destruct. Society needs no more thermometers, monitoring the ups and downs of our present social climate. It needs instead a thermostat, something which by its very presence will regulate a culture in crisis. Such is the God-given role of the church.

It is said that when Horatio Nelson found two officers arguing on the deck of his ship, moments before the Battle of Trafalgar, he pointed to the French fleet on the horizon and said: 'Gentlemen, there's your enemy.' Meekness is that God-given ability to harness – not suppress – our impulses. In this way meekness becomes controlled strength. 'Blessed is the man who has learnt how to live within the reins in life, who, by the indwelling power of the Holy Spirit, is entirely self-controlled.'

Possessing the earth

Very few modern-day go-getters would ever consider, let alone propound, meekness as a vital ingredient for success. Such a philosophy would be viewed as anathema to those who are today so success-orientated. Yet Jesus advocated such a quality as a key component to becoming a winner. 'Blessed, to be congratulated, are the meek, for they will inherit the earth' (Matthew 5:5 paraphrased).

Carl Sanburg described Abraham Lincoln as 'a man of steel and velvet'. Mark van Doren says of the American President: 'To me, Lincoln seems, in some ways, the most interesting man who ever lived. He was gentle, but this gentleness was combined with a terrific toughness, an iron strength.'[4] Such is the twofold nature of those who claim to be 'partakers of the divine nature' (2 Peter 1:4 NASB), those who desire to 'fulfil' or 'fill full' their God-given destiny in life.

This promise of 'inheriting the earth' is said to derive from Psalm 37: 'A little while, and the wicked will be no more; though you look for them, they will not be found. But the meek will inherit the land and enjoy great peace' (verses 10–11). The psalm describes a people who are not in a position to overcome the power of the wicked and need therefore to rely on God. They in turn are promised that God will establish them in such a way as to inherit what is redemptively their inheritance, that is 'the land'.

Kingdom worldview

'The earth is the Lord's,' says the Psalmist (Psalm 24:1), and God's promise of the land of Canaan to the people of Israel was that they would 'possess their land' (Leviticus 20:24). This foreshadowed God's promise of the earth to the people of faith (see also Romans 4:13). Here, then, is a key issue, a crucial attitude for those who want to be involved in advancing God's kingdom on earth.

Because this promise involves the earth, we must guard against the parochial and maintain a kingdom worldview:

- The earth is God's (Psalm 24:1).
- It will be filled with his glory (Habakkuk 2:14).
- Christ overcame the world and we are 'in Christ' (John 16:33; 2 Corinthians 5:17).
- All authority in heaven and on earth belong to Christ and to us who are in Christ (Matthew 28:18).
- If we are meek we will inherit the earth (Matthew 5:5).

Much of today's theology sees an end-time church locked into a type of 'Custer's-last-stand' mentality. According to this viewpoint the church will remain a minority with little to look forward to and few resources left with which to combat the satanic onslaught. As a result, the church longingly waits for the coming of Jesus Christ and heaven's hosts as some kind of divine cavalry with trumpets blasting and sabres glistening, coming to rescue a defeated church. Yet Paul, in writing to the church at Ephesus, reminds them of the day when Christ will come for 'a radiant church, without stain or wrinkle or any other blemish, but holy and blameless' (Ephesians 5:27).

God's purpose remains unchanged from the beginning. He commanded men and women to 'be fruitful and increase in number; fill the earth and subdue it' (Genesis 1:28). Our task is to work with God to bring it about so that we can enter our promised inheritance – and meekness is fundamental to our success.

Making it happen

When God's will is done, his kingdom has come. But before his will can affect this generation, it must affect me personally. I must align myself with what is 'good, pleasing and perfect', that is, with 'God's will' (Romans 12:2).

A man may have the desire to line up his will with God's but, as much as he tries, he cannot do it in his own strength: 'For what I want to do I do not do, but what I hate I do' (Romans 7:15). Like an unbroken horse, the human will, motivated by its natural instincts, stubbornly pursues a course of action with little thought for the consequences. It resists all attempts by external influences to redirect its path; it is doing what comes naturally. Like the proverbial donkey the will is strong, stubborn and selfish (see Jeremiah 2:20–24; Isaiah 1:2–4).

In contrast, God's will was perfectly expressed by Jesus, who could say: 'I always do what pleases (the Father)' (John 8:29).

Yet, 'although he was a son, he learned obedience from what he suffered' (Hebrews 5:8). Jesus' success in always doing the Father's will came out of a learning process that included the personal inconvenience and pain of rejecting temptation and obeying God. As we seek to harness our will to do God's will, we find in Christ a perfect example to follow.

Without the redemptive work of the Holy Spirit, the will of the unregenerate person is primed and ready to self-destruct. It is a condition symptomatic of a people who 'die for lack of discipline' (Proverbs 5:12–13,23). Only through the miracle of new birth can humankind become 'a new creation' in which 'the old has gone, the new has come' (2 Corinthians 5:17). Therefore, as 'participators in the divine nature' regenerate man takes control of every natural desire and, reflecting the nature of Christ, submits to God's purposes, praying: 'Father . . . not as I will, but as you will' (Matthew 26:39).

Meekness is not weakness. Neither does it mean being belligerent, fighting for what we want. True meekness has a serving attitude and a willingness to submit to authority, to allow the dealings of God and people in our lives without retaliation. It is not bucking authority or reacting in such a way as to cry out: 'Get off my back!'

Trust and obey

The Greek word for obedience is *hupoakoe*, *hupo* meaning 'under' and *akouo* meaning 'to hear'. The act of obedience is characteristic of someone who has understood the principle of authority. As we obey God's Word we are putting ourselves voluntarily under his protection and authority. We hear and obey his every word.

Obedience is a 'chain of command' word, whereas disobedience implies a mis-hearing. The Greek word here is *parakoe*, *para* meaning 'side' and *akouo* 'to hear'. It suggests that to disobey is to move from our rightful position of dependence and honour under our heavenly Father's authority, so as to come alongside/against him, a place of independence and therefore insurrection. It could also be seen as a position of seeming equality, a human endeavour to parallel our thoughts with God's thoughts and our ways with his.

Self-control

Aubrey Andelin writes: 'The foundation of a noble character is self-mastery. It is the key to applying any virtue in which we may be lacking and will carry us to our greatest objective – becoming a perfect individual. Self-mastery is the means whereby we apply knowledge of basic principles, overcome weakness, conquer appetites and passions, and devote ourselves to duty and reach our objectives . . . Self-mastery is the motivating force whereby we reach upward.

> "He who rules within himself and rules his passions,
> desires and fears is more than a king."
>
> Milton.'[5]

'Better a patient man than a warrior, a man who controls his temper than one who takes a city' (Proverbs 16:32). Any leader who wants to control must himself be controlled. Those who want to exercise authority must themselves be under authority.

Alexander the Great, one of history's most famous inspirers and motivators, led his army of thousands across desert and mountain terrain. Yet his ability to lead became somewhat compromised when in a drunken stupor: the young king lost his temper and in the ensuing brawl he speared his friend Cleitus to death.

To take control, I must be under control. Kingdom rule must begin in me before it can conquer others.

Notes

[1] Cleon L Rogers Jr, *A Linguistic Key to the Greek New Testament* (Zondervan, 1980).

[2] Barclay, *The Daily Study Bible* (St Andrew's Press, 1976)

[3] W E Vine, *Expository Dictionary of New Testament Words* (Oliphants, 1969).

[4] Aubrey Andelin, *Man of Steel and Velvet* (Bantam Books, 1983).

[5] Andelin, op. cit.

REDEMPTIVE ATTITUDE No 3

'Blessed are the meek,
for they shall inherit
the earth.'

'A life submitted to the
master's reins, one whose
strength of character is
harnessed and focused
towards establishing the
government of God in himself/herself
and in the lives of others.'

CHAPTER SIX

THE LAW OF APPETITE

*'Let those [of us] who are spiritually mature and
full-grown have this mind and hold these
convictions, and if in any respect you have a
different attitude of mind, God will make that
clear to you also.'*

Philippians 3:15 [AMPLIFIED BIBLE]

In a short public life that lasted only twelve years, Martin Luther King managed to change the course of social history. As a hero of the civil rights movement, he championed a cause that was to transform the southern states of America.

King advocated a non-violent approach to public protest. He became one of America's leading lights during the dark days of segregation. With the powerful eloquence of a master orator Martin Luther King holds a place unprecedented in the history of black America.

On the evening of 3 April 1968 King spoke to a strike rally in Memphis, delivering one of his most famous speeches. He said:

'We have been forced to a point where we're going to have to grapple with the problems that men have been trying to grapple with through history, but the demands didn't force them to do it. Survival demands that we grapple with them. Men, for years now, have been talking about war and peace. But now no longer can they just talk about it. It is no longer a choice between violence and non-violence in this world, it's non-violence or non-existence . . .

'Let us rise up tonight with a greater readiness. Let us stand with a greater determination. And let us move on in these powerful days, these days of challenge, to make America a better nation. And I want to thank God, once more, for allowing me to be here with you . . .

'I don't know what will happen now. We've got some difficult days ahead. But it doesn't matter with me now, because I've been to the mountain top. And I don't mind. Like anybody, I would like to live a long life; longevity has its place. But I'm not concerned about that now. I just want to do God's will. And he's allowed me to go up to the mountain. And I've looked over. And I've seen the promised land. I may not get there with you. But I want you to know tonight that we as a people will get to the promised land. And I'm happy tonight, I'm not worried about anything. I'm not fearing any man. Mine eyes have seen the glory of the coming of the Lord.'[1]

The following evening, on his way to a friend's house for dinner, he paused on the balcony outside his motel to talk to staff members. Suddenly, without warning, an assassin's bullet hit him. Moments later, Martin Luther King was dead.

I've been to the mountain top

Like Moses before him, Martin Luther King had been to the top of his mountain. He had caught a glimpse of what for him was the promised land. It was a land where 'the sons of former slaves and the sons of former slave owners will be able to sit down together at the table of brotherhood'. It was a land where injustice and oppression would give way to freedom and justice; where men would not be judged by the colour of their skin, but by the content of their character.

Martin Luther King had his dream, but the church must have its reality. Only those who have ascended the hill of the Lord and tasted God's righteousness are adequately prepared to confront the injustice and oppression in today's world. The church has first to learn how to rely on God and maintain the spiritual high ground before she can adequately relate to the social dilemmas of humankind. 'Blessed and fortunate and happy and spiritually prosperous . . . are those who hunger and thirst for righteousness . . . for they shall be completely satisfied!' (Matthew 5:6 Amplified Bible).

We have now arrived at the high-point of all that Jesus taught about attitudes. Having established our base camp on the nursery slopes of 'poverty of spirit', we have plotted a course that has taken us through the valley of 'spiritual sensitivity'. Now that we have faced the challenge of 'meekness', we are ready for the final push towards the summit of 'righteousness'. This is the place for which all men and women must long.

Once we have found the peace and satisfaction that only a right relationship with God can give, we must maintain our spiritual appetite. In this way we hold the spiritual high ground of being and doing right. From this vantage point we can view the world from God's perspective, enjoying the clear air and sunlight that accompanies a right relationship with him. Only when we have experienced mercy can we 'show mercy'. Only when we have made peace can we become a 'peacemaker' (see Diagram 1).

Heavenly octave

Now seems a good time to look again at these eight attitudes in their complete setting. We can view the 'mathematical' or 'musical' structure of what F W Boreham calls 'The Heavenly Octave'. When we listen to good music, few of us analyse its construction, but a quality composition bears such a critical examination. In these eight Beatitudes there is both progression and balance.

The first four attitudes suggest four upward steps in preparing the heart for God's fullness. Each of these inward works of grace involves God's dealings with people. They teach us to rely on God rather than ourselves:

1. I am absolutely empty and destitute without God.
2. I am utterly devastated by my sinful waywardness.
3. I want all my natural strengths tamed and harnessed.
4. I am desperate for all that God has for me.

Taken together these attitudes characterise a people who are looking to God as their only source of supply, spiritual wealth, strength, power and righteousness drawn from heaven's resources.

This is the absolute opposite of a self-satisfied, complacent, lethargic attitude. It is an angle of approach to life symptomatic of the spiritually stagnant, those into whom the springs of Holy Spirit life have ceased to flow (John 7:37–39). Consequently, few drink from their well.

Righteousness revisited

The pivotal point of this whole teaching on attitudes is the issue of righteousness. It is crucial, therefore, that we understand what is meant by this biblical term.

Righteousness means that all my sin was 'imputed' to Jesus (put into his account – 2 Corinthians 5:21) so that he could take it away through the cross. When I receive him by faith as my Lord and Saviour, all his rightness is imputed to me. My one-time spiritually bankrupt account is now accredited with the righteousness of Jesus Christ. He has paid the bill in full by his act of sacrifice, setting my balance sheet in credit with his goodness, virtue, perfection and righteousness.

Righteousness means a life of integrity, governed by truth and honesty, committed to godliness and set free from selfish desires and vested interest. While the Christian's legal standing is one of being right, the righteousness of God by its very nature also involves doing right. Righteousness is a quality of life. If it is not social in its outworking it is not true godly righteousness. John Stott, writing about Charles Finney's views on social reform, says: 'Social involvement was both the child of evangelical religion and the twin sister of evangelism.'[2]

Unless today's church revisits the issues of moral as well as legal righteousness – *doing* as well as *being* righteous – she will not be heard in the debate on social injustice and human oppression. Each believer must therefore maintain his or her appetite for righteousness.

The Apostle Paul's hungering and thirsting for righteousness was a deep desire to know more of the person and power of Christ. It is an attitude he later commends to the whole church: 'Let us therefore, as many as are perfect, have this attitude; and if in anything you have a different attitude, God will reveal that also to you' (Philippians 3:15 NASB).

This attitude is at the core of kingdom life. It is crystallised in that most central of commands recorded in Matthew's account of the Sermon on the Mount: 'Seek first his kingdom and his righteousness, and all these things will be given to you as well' (Matthew 6:33). The kingdom of God is 'not a matter of eating and drinking, but of righteousness, peace and joy in the Holy Spirit' (Romans 14:17).

When we hunger and thirst for true righteousness we desire to live free from the old self-life and to express the divine nature in all we say and do; 'to put on the new self, created to be like God in true righteousness and holiness' (Ephesians 4:24). It is not that I need Jesus to do any more *for* me – his redemptive work is complete – it is that I need him to do more *in* me.

Maintaining the moral high ground

As Jesus in his Sermon on the Mount develops his theme of hungering and thirsting, he specifically highlights areas of righteousness which the Christian must hunger after. For example, he speaks of moral purity, verbal honesty and covenantal loyalty.

Moral purity (Matthew 5:27–30)

These verses graphically describe God's kingdom as a radical form of government. We live in a promiscuous society in which any kind of sexual perversion seems not only acceptable but desirable. The citizen who lives under divine government must hunger for moral purity.

The word 'lustfully' is a powerful word, and is used to describe 'uncontrolled desire'. It is a renegade desire that causes us to look wantonly at others, reach out and touch, take or taste what is not rightfully ours. Such a desire must be rounded up and brought under control.

'If your right eye causes you to sin, gouge it out and throw it away . . . And if your right hand causes you to sin, cut it off and throw it away' (Matthew 5:29–30). The cure is radical, the alternative disastrous. Spiritual surgery, no matter how painful, must be applied. To change the metaphor but stay with the principle: 'We demolish arguments and every pretension that sets itself up against the knowledge of God, and we take captive every thought to make it obedient to Christ' (2 Corinthians 10:5).

In his book *The King and You*, Bob Mumford says: 'We know that Jesus' words are not to be taken literally, for that other eye can prove offensive; and the left hand may reach out to "touch" equally as greedily as the right one. Jesus is saying that if there is lust in your heart, you have two problems: the eye and the hand. Both are under control of the heart. If you have the temptation to lust . . . get rid of that eye! If you have the temptation to touch things that don't belong to you . . . get rid of that hand! For these temptations will eventually lead to the destruction of the whole body. This may include your business, your marriage (or prospects of marriage), your health, your spiritual progress – total!'[3]

Verbal honesty (Matthew 5:33–37)

We are talking here about maintaining an appetite for verbal honesty, a desire to hold a godly position in all our daily conversations. Verbal integrity involves obeying Paul's teaching to the Colossians when he says: 'Rid yourselves of all such things as these: anger, rage, malice, slander and filthy language from your lips. Do not lie to each other' (Colossians 3:8–9; compare Ephesians 4:23–25).

It also means avoiding the temptation to exaggerate what is factually true so as to impress, or becoming manipulative in our talk so as to persuade others. It includes being constructive and not destructive, open and honest in speaking with others. It is making sure that our word is our bond.

Words carry the potential of both good and evil. You can become 'snared by the words of your own mouth' (Proverbs 6:1–5 RAV). Because the Lord knows our words before they are spoken (Psalm 139:4), our prayer is: 'Set a guard over my mouth, O Lord . . . [so that] the words of my lips and the meditations of my heart may be pleasing' to the Lord (see Psalm 141:3; 19:14).

Covenantal loyalty (Matthew 5:21–26; 18:15)

Anger as a God-given emotion is not necessarily wrong. God gets angry but does not sin. Therefore righteous anger has its place. But the crime here is anger without cause: 'Whosoever is angry with his brother without cause shall be in danger of the judgement' (Matthew 5:22 KJV). That would imply that there are times when anger is justified. In his letter to the Ephesians, Paul wrote: '"In your anger do not sin": Do not let the sun go down while you are still angry, and do not give the devil a foothold' (Ephesians 4:26–27).

The whole sequence of events here is to do with interpersonal relationships, and the question is: 'Is my anger rooted in a just and righteous cause? Or am I reacting because my personal feelings, pride or prejudices have been affected?' Let the indwelling Spirit of God judge our motives. Whether we bring a judgement or not, judgement will come. Anger without just cause will produce an unrighteous reaction. Left without judgement it will mature into revenge.

Covenantal loyalty demands that I do all I can (Romans 12:18–19) to bring a resolve to the issue at hand. Where I have offended a brother, or he has offended me, the responsibility is always mine. 'Therefore if . . . your brother has something against you . . . go and be reconciled to your brother' (Matthew 5:23–24). 'If your brother sins against you, go and show him his fault, just between the two of you' (Matthew 18:15).

The relationship of commitment between members of the body of Christ demands that we resolve issues and not allow them to fester. How often have Christians refused to live according to this simple principle, attending the same place of worship yet refusing to resolve their differences? Hungering and thirsting for righteousness involves not saying behind my brother's back what I have not said to his face.

Righteousness exalts a nation. The heroes of this generation must therefore ascend the hill of the Lord. They must maintain a 'righteousness consciousness' with clean hands and a pure heart, in and through their ongoing relationship with a righteous God. Then, having tasted righteousness, they need to maintain a spiritual hunger for it, avoiding at all cost those situations that would spoil their appetite.

From this vantage point we see social issues from God's perspective and are equipped to become merciful. We can empathise with people's spiritual and social need, and where necessary we can make and maintain God's peace.

Intense hunger and thirst

Hunger and thirst are fundamental to sustaining natural life and growth. They are also vital in the spiritual realm. If people falter on this angle of approach it is a sign of spiritual disorder which, left unchecked, will prove disastrous.

When we hunger and thirst for righteousness we express the degree of longing essential for our fulfilment in the Christian life. On the natural level, intense hunger and thirst are virtually unknown to people in the West. Our limited frame of reference is a hindrance to grasping their meaning. The Holy Spirit, however, can enable us to 'know' something that 'surpasses knowledge' (see Ephesians 3:19).

Paul chooses his words carefully here. The normal Greek word for hunger and thirst would indicate the need for a piece of bread or a glass of water. But the word used here implies 'an intense hunger and thirst for all that is available'. This is no partial appetite, a spiritual peckishness easily satisfied with a snack. Rather, it is an intense hunger and thirst.

In his book *God's Chosen Fast*, Arthur Wallis distinguishes between 'appetite' and 'hunger': 'It is doubtful whether the average individual, reared in our well-fed Western civilisation, knows much of genuine hunger. Hunger is a cry from the whole body stemming from need. We might say, then, that mere appetite relates to the immediate "want" of the stomach, true hunger to the real "need" of the body.'[4]

When the prodigal son began to be 'in need' (Luke 15:14), he turned to the pig swill. When he was absolutely 'starving' (v17), he turned to his father, whose servants had more than enough.

The attitude before us, therefore, is no momentary desire, passing fancy or whim. It is a deep need affecting our whole being; it is an intense hunger and thirst for all that is available in Christ Jesus. When I find nothing that can fully satisfy my inner longing I approach the God of 'much more' (Romans 5:9–10,15,17 NASB).

The account of famine-stricken Samaria and the radical action of some lepers who risked all for food (see 2 Kings 6:24–25; 7:3–16) teaches us some vital keys to true hunger and thirst. Deep hunger and thirst is a powerful motivator. Their hunger propelled them into action. In the same way, a spiritual hunger will:

- Focus your vision.
- Rid you of the unnecessary. Many people will remember the harrowing reports on TV of families making mammoth journeys in order to escape famine, the route marked by their belongings left beside the road. Things once thought vital to life now become secondary and unimportant. A true spiritual thirst for God will not only crystallise your vision, but also rid you of things once eagerly sought after.
- Sharpen your desires.
- Move you out of mediocrity.
- Make you a risk-taker.
- Cause you to speak up.
- Result in your knowing fulfilment (Isaiah 44:3–5; John 7:37–39).

One wise observer has said: 'Without a healthy appetite, mealtimes become a drudgery instead of a delight.' Without this angle of approach to the things of God, Bible study, church gatherings, prayer and intercession, life becomes a chore. When we hunger and thirst for God we have reached the pinnacle of our whole approach to life. Peter warns of five things guaranteed to ruin your hungering and thirsting for God:

- Malice – When I want to hurt you.
- Deceit – Twisting the truth.
- Hypocrisy – Two faced.
- Envy – Jealous of others.
- Slander – Talking behind someone's back.

How do we regain our appetite? The sequence in which this series of attitudes is written is, I believe, a clear guide to the way to create as well as maintain a healthy spiritual desire. If we have lost our spiritual eagerness we need to return to the issue of spiritual poverty. After visiting base camp, we must allow the Holy Spirit to sensitise us to those things that have violated the government of God in our lives. Then, by allowing the dealings of God and people to work for good in our lives, we will begin to hunger and thirst for the things of God.

A healthy spiritual appetite also includes:

- A hunger for God – Psalm 42:1–2; 63:1.
- A thirst for truth – Psalm 119:129–136.
- A zeal to fulfil God's will – John 4:34; Titus 2:14.
- A longing for the presence and power of God – John 7:37–39; 1 Corinthians 14:1; Isaiah 55:1.

Complete satisfaction

Those who 'hunger and thirst for righteousness' will enjoy the promised result: 'They will be completely satisfied.' The same word 'satisfied' is used to describe the result of Jesus' feeding of the four thousand: 'The people ate and were satisfied. Afterwards the disciples picked up seven basketfuls of broken pieces that were left over' (Mark 8:8).

They were satisfied and there was plenty to spare, because God's provision is always abundant. In Christ we, like the twelve disciples, tap into a divine source of supply that will not only meet our immediate needs but provide more besides. The phrase 'that were left over' denotes 'abundance' and is the same word that is used in 2 Corinthians 8:13–14: 'Your abundance may be a supply' (KJV). In Christ Jesus we find the source of 'life . . . to the full' (John 10:10). 'He satisfies the thirsty and fills the hungry with good things' (Psalm 107:9).

Abundant life is having enough to meet my needs and more besides to minister to the needs of others. It is an abundance of energy, time, finance, ability and resource that is sufficient for what I need and enough to give to others. Finding and maintaining this level of fulfilment must surely be the goal of all humankind.

Flowing out to the nations

How crucial it us for us to experience true spiritual fullness before we seek to approach the next four attitudes! From here on we will be called to minister to others out of what we have entered into and enjoyed in God. Being a 'person who shows mercy' and a 'peacemaker' demands that we have first experienced true 'mercy' and 'peace'. Only if we have been made 'pure' within can we hope to serve others from a pure motive and maintain a right attitude in the face of real opposition.

After we have been filled with a 'good measure, pressed down, shaken together and running over' (Luke 6:38), we are able to flow out to the nations. We can show mercy because we have tasted God's mercy. We can make peace because we have met with the God of peace who has accredited our account with his peace and righteousness.

Increasing levels of expectations

Small-mindedness, self-limitation and an apathetic attitude – such things are not the mind-set of a winner. Winners are people who, on the basis of what they believe to be true, maintain a positive attitude of high expectation in the face of all opposition.

DeVern Fromke comments: 'In each generation God always has had those men whose framework of vision reached beyond the general consciousness to see God's larger purpose. They lived and breathed with a divine destiny consciousness imparted by God. Such men always moved beyond the narrow vision of their day.'[5]

When we hunger and thirst we have an angle of approach to life in which on the one hand we desire what is rightfully ours and on the other we show a determination to achieve it. The reality of outward circumstances does not deter winners. They recognise their present limitations and maintain a high level of expectation.

Paul writes of 'the field God has assigned to us . . . our area of activity' (2 Corinthians 10:12–18). The word 'area' can also be translated 'sphere' and is defined as: 'definitely bounded or fixed space within the limits of which one's power or influence is confined; the province assigned to one; one's sphere of activity'.[6]

The word 'sphere' was used by the Greeks to describe a reed, spear, staff or measuring rod that measured the distance attained by an athlete at the Olympic Games. Winners would recognise the measured limits of their particular running lane and would not go beyond those limits. To do so was to risk possible disqualification, making the months of relentless preparation pointless.

In the same way, the Apostle Paul recognised his God-given limitations. Rather than allowing such to become a mental restriction, his attitude was one of hungering and thirsting for all that was rightfully his. We, too, set up mental landmarks and mark what we believe is redemptively ours. Then in faith we move out to occupy our God-given inheritance.

Abraham 'grew strong in faith . . . being fully assured that what [God] had promised, he was able also to perform' (Romans 4:20–21 NASB). Joseph maintained a positive attitude in the midst of a series of restrictive circumstances. Whether in the pit or prison he was a 'success in everything he did' (Genesis 39:3, 23). The same attitude can be seen in such people as David (Psalm 27; 1 Samuel 17:45–47), Joshua (Joshua 14:8) and Naomi (Ruth 4:14–15). What I believe concerning myself, God, people, objects or events will determine how I live. Beliefs result in expectation, which in turn affects my level of achievement.

When Winston Churchill was invited to address a graduation ceremony at a school in England, he amazed his audience by giving them the shortest graduation speech they had ever heard. Looking across a sea of expectant faces that eagerly awaited those pearls of wisdom that only Winston could bring, he began to speak with the authority of one whose words had inspired thousands:

'Never give up! Never give up! Never ever give up!'

He then sat down. Although the speech was incredibly short, he had made his point. Not one student would ever forget that lesson for life – a key phrase for all who want to be winners.

Thomas Edison experienced thousands of failures before inventing the light bulb. The Wright brothers had to persist in the midst of countless failures before finding a method for getting an airplane into the sky. None of us are exempt from the pressures, failures and set-backs in life. No wonder, then, that a determined attitude is vital if we are to attain the attainable.

Notes

[1] Coretta Scott King, *The Words of Martin Luther King* (William Collins, 1983).

[2] John Stott, *Involvement: Being a Responsible Christian in a Non-Christian Society* (Revell, 1985).

[3] Bob Mumford, *The King and You* (Revell, 1974).

[4] Arthur Wallis, *God's Chosen Fast* (Kingsway, 1978).

[5] DeVern Fromke, *Unto Full Stature* (CLC, 1965).

[6] Joseph H Thayer, *Greek-English Lexicon of the New Testament* (Baker, 1986).

REDEMPTIVE ATTITUDE No 4

*'Blessed are those who hunger
and thirst for righteousness,
for they will be filled.'*

'Maintaining a healthy appetite
for being and doing what
is right in the sight of God.'

CHAPTER SEVEN

GET OUT OF JAIL FREE

'A relaxed attitude lengthens a man's life;
jealousy rots it away.'

Proverbs 14:30 [LIVING BIBLE]

'I've been to the top of the mountain!' Hungry and thirsty for God we have discovered the secret of true success. But, having experienced fullness and the joy of seeing our one-time bankrupt account accredited with the rightness of Jesus, how easy it would be to become spiritually smug and self-satisfied:

- Arrogantly building a monument so as to commemorate this momentous moment.
- Settling down and warming ourselves from the glow of theological truth.
- Continually reflecting on a former life and the depths from which God has delivered us.
- Locking ourselves into a religious merry-go-round of predictable routines.
- Becoming infatuated with nostalgic songs, religious platitudes and the habitual listening to a three-point homily.

In the midst of the brilliance of Christ's transfiguration, Peter's impetuous response was to build something, to put up a tent so as to contain and commemorate this important concept (see Mark 9:2–6). History teaches us that God's people have a tendency to pitch camp around one aspect of God's progressive truth, settle into a spiritual comfort zone and become entrenched in tradition, unwilling to move on. But Christ will not return until the 'restoration of all things about which God spoke by the mouth of his holy prophets' (Acts 3:21 NASB).

126

Peter was forgetting that God was no longer confined to a tabernacle or temple; the Word had become flesh and was dwelling among men. When referring back to this incident, John, with a different perspective from Peter, wrote: 'We proclaim to you what we have seen and heard, so that you also may have fellowship with us' (1 John 1:3).

We have been to the mountain and, like Moses, caught a glimpse of the eternal plan. We must now 'go and make disciples of all nations, baptising them in the name of the Father and of the Son and of the Holy Spirit, and teaching them to obey everything I have commanded you' (Matthew 28:19–20). It is both pharisaical and hypocritical to imbibe a self-righteous attitude by which we say, 'God, I thank you that I am not like other men' (Luke 18:11) . By its very nature, righteousness is relational. Although it involves primarily 'being right', righteousness includes the concept of 'doing right'.

When I was working as a carpenter, I was involved in a kitchen refit in the north of England at the home of a keen road cyclist. The house was so littered with the various trappings to do with the sport that there was little room for anything else. I was interested to know more about a hobby for which the man of the house clearly lived and breathed. I asked his wife how her husband managed to pursue his interest amidst the harsh realities of a northern winter.

'Well,' she said, 'each Sunday morning without fail he's up at the crack of dawn and dressed in his riding gear ready to go.'

'Even when there's snow on the ground?' I asked.

'Oh, yes,' she replied.

I was impressed. Such dedication to a sport during the bitter cold of a Yorkshire winter is, to say the least, commendable.

Seeing the look of admiration on my face, she was quick to put me right. 'Oh, no, you don't understand. Once he puts on his cycling kit he brings his bike into the living room, puts on the gas fire, gets out his cycling magazines and sits down in the chair to dream of the day when he can take to the road again.'

The harsh reality of Jesus' words in Matthew 25:14–30 concerning those who, having received, sat back idly awaiting the king's return, should awaken us all to the needs of the world. Those who are truly righteous are to feed the hungry, give drink to the thirsty, open their doors to the stranger, clothe and care for the needy.

As someone has well said: 'An individual has not started living until he can rise above the narrow confines of his individualistic concerns to the broader concerns of all humanity. Every man must decide whether he will walk in the light of creative altruism [regard for others as a principle of action] or the darkness of destructive selfishness. This is the judgement. Life's most persistent and urgent question is, "What are you doing for others?"'[1]

Christianity must break out of bricks and mortar. It must feel the draught and harsh realities of a bleak social winter that causes millions to die of malnutrition and the possibility of whole nations being wiped out through AIDS. It must take on flesh and blood and address the relevant issues of the day. The church cannot remain silent on such issues as violence, war, racism, inner-city crime, drugs, poverty, child abuse and homelessness.

Life's harsh realities must not become no-go areas for the church. True Christianity belongs at the heart of humanity, and the church has to decide what sort of world she wants to belong to. 'The next ten years will decide the shape of the 21st century. They may decide the future of the earth as a habitation for human beings.'[2]

Be-attitudes

The first four redemptive attitudes deal primarily with our learning to rely on God. In contrast, the remaining four are to do with the way we relate to people in the light of what we have received. The natural consequence of experiencing heaven's fullness is a life on earth which overflows to others. Once we have tasted the righteousness of Christ, our natural instinct is to do right, to 'show mercy' and to 'make peace' from 'motives which are pure and clear'.

The giving of the law to Moses is to the Old Testament what the Sermon on the Mount is to the New. The Ten Commandments have four laws that relate to people's relationship with God and six that concentrate on his interpersonal relationships with each other. Taking up this point, Paul writes: 'The entire law is summed up in a single command: "Love your neighbour as yourself"' (Galatians 5:14).

The four Beatitudes we are now going to study highlight what would be better termed 'be-attitudes' – that is, they focus on our being rather than our doing. These are not natural tendencies, present in some people and absent in others. They are attitudes rooted in Christ and, for the child of God, as natural as apples on an apple tree! The fact is, we are 'partakers of the divine nature, having escaped the corruption that is in the world through lust' (2 Peter 1:4 KJV).

God's kingdom is not so much a question of *doing* as *being*: 'The kingdom of God is not a matter of eating and drinking, but of righteousness, peace and joy in the Holy Spirit, because anyone who serves Christ in this way is pleasing to God and approved by men' (Romans 14:17–18). And the kind of 'righteousness' from which the 'peace' and 'joy' issue is relational.

Although I know very few millionaires, those I do know never seem to find it necessary to prove to anyone their abundant wealth. They go about their daily lives secure in the knowledge of who they are and what is available to them. That's how citizens of the King need to behave. We can live secure in the truth of who we are 'in Christ'. We don't have to struggle or strive to be someone, but by faith we 'count [ourselves] dead to sin' (Romans 6:11), and walk in the good of our new-found freedom.

When we are poor in spirit, our sufficiency is in God. We are spiritually sensitive, knowing God's heart. By channelling his mighty strength through our every ability, we seek for more of his rightness to be worked in and through us. From this vantage point God's life naturally flows out from us. As natural as the law of gravity is to humans, and the law of aerodynamics is to fledglings, so are the following attitudes to citizens of God's kingdom.

What does mercy mean?

'Blessed – happy, to be envied, and spiritually prosperous . . . are the merciful, for they shall obtain mercy!' (Matthew 5:7 Amplified Bible). When we have experienced God's mercy in Christ we are adequately equipped to 'show mercy' to others. 'Be merciful, just as your Father is merciful' (Luke 6:36).

By its very definition mercy assumes a need in the one who receives it and the resources adequate to meet that need in the one who shows it. Now that we have tapped into the one who is 'rich in mercy' (Ephesians 2:4), we are able to show the same compassion as Christ did.

Showing mercy is not just an emotional spasm of pity given spontaneously. Rather, it is a redemptive attitude by which we deliberately identify ourselves with a person's situation, be it positive or negative. It is sympathy in the real sense of the word. The word 'sympathy' is derived from two Greek words, *syn*, which means 'together with' and *paschein*, which means 'to experience or to suffer'; or 'to be affected with the same feeling as another'.

Paul describes to the Hebrews the present-day ministry of Christ. We are to approach 'the throne of grace' with confidence

because we have an advocate who is 'touched with the feeling of infirmities' (Hebrews 4:15 KJV). Christ is able to sympathise with us and we can be assured of receiving 'mercy . . . to help us in our time of need' (v16).

True sympathy in its literal sense is to experience something with another person, to empathise with people in both the good and the bad. Paul encouraged the Christians at Corinth to sympathise with their fellow believers: 'If one part [of the body] suffers, every part suffers with it; if one part is honoured, every part rejoices with it' (1 Corinthians 12:26). It is a deliberate and determined identification with someone, a heartfelt desire to see things from their perspective and to feel what they feel. It is to 'rejoice with those who rejoice, and weep with those who weep' (Romans 12:15 NASB).

To prevent sympathy becoming a sloppy sentimentality, we should recognise that this angle of approach to life does not mean:

- Feeling sorry for people and joining in their 'pity party'.
- Letting unrepentant people off the hook when they have violated God's Word. Mercy is not an easygoing spirit so that we overlook issues of truth. Mercy and truth are often linked together in Scripture. Abraham showed mercy in securing Lot even though he had wronged him (Genesis 14:1–16). Joseph showed mercy to his brothers (Genesis 50:15–21). Moses prayed for Miriam's healing in spite of her rebellion (Numbers 12:13). David showed mercy by sparing Saul's life (1 Samuel 24:5–7).
- Easing the pain but ignoring its cause.
- Being kind in the wrong way and at the wrong time. For instance, when Jesus visited the home of Martha and Mary (Luke 10:38–42), Mary understood that Jesus wanted peace and identified herself with his need. Martha, on the other hand, wanted to bless and impress. Both showed sympathy

but only Mary empathised with the needs of Jesus. How often we offer kindness in our way and on our terms, whether the other party likes it or not.

When the widow's son died in Zarephath (1 Kings 17:7–24), in her frustration the widow accused Elijah. He responded with love and understanding, not logic and biblical principles. Later, when he himself was suffering from nervous exhaustion following the victory on Mount Carmel, he begged to die (1 Kings 19:3–4). Jezebel would have gladly done the job for him, but God empathised with him. Rather than pointing out Elijah's unreasonableness, God sent an angel to feed him supernaturally. Having shown mercy and allowed Elijah to rest, God later cornered him in a cave and applied truth with his various acts of kindness (1 Kings 19:9–18).

Mercy is more than offering encouraging words to people who feel depressed or giving advice to needy people. It is an identification with a need so that you feel what the other person feels, you see and hear what that person sees and hears. It is primarily a decision of the will, to do whatever is necessary to bring a righteous resolve to the situation. It is to see the need and by God's grace do the right thing at the right time in the right way. It is having a true redemptive attitude in our dealings with other people.

Showing mercy can involve:

- Identifying a person's need for them.
- Specific acts of kindness. The Good Samaritan is an example of someone who showed mercy (see Luke 10:30–37). While the representatives of orthodox religion passed by the wounded man, the Samaritan 'saw him . . . took pity on him . . . bandaged his wounds, pouring on oil and wine. Then he put the man on his own donkey, brought him to an inn and took care of him.' Mercy, according to Dr Martyn Lloyd-Jones,

means: 'A sense of pity, plus a desire to relieve the suffering
. . . It is pity, plus action.'[3]

- Being quick to forgive an offence.
- Releasing people from what you could sometimes rightfully
  demand. Philemon owed his life to the apostle Paul, who now
  asked him to reciprocate mercy by treating his runaway slave
  as he would Paul (Philemon 17).
- Being honest enough to expose root issues and helping people
  to work through them.

'Incarnational theology'

While on a ten-month lecture tour of America, Nico and Ellen
Smith heard Henri Nouwen talking on the subject of incarna-
tional theology. What Nouwen said made a lasting impression
on both Nico and Ellen. Nouwen explained his theory: 'If you
really want to minister to the poor, you have to live as they live.
You have to be one of them, to experience the same problems,
to live the same life, to share the same distresses. Only then can
you truly identify with those you have come to serve.'

Hooked by what they heard, the Smiths determined to look
further into this teaching. In their search they came across a
book by John Perkins, a black pastor brought up in the deep
South of the USA. Perkins had been beaten almost to death in
police cells during the 1970s for his work in the civil rights
movement. Nico went through the book entitled *Justice for All*,
marking passages that underlined what Henri Nouwen had
taught. They included the following:

'If we are going to be the body of Christ, shouldn't we do as
he did? He didn't commute daily from heaven to earth to minister to us. Nor did he set up a mission compound which would
make him immune to our problems. No, he became flesh and
lived among us.

'God didn't have to become a man to find out what our needs

were; but we needed him to become man so that we would know he knew our needs. Because he became one of us, we could be sure he understood.

'An outsider can seldom know the needs of the community well enough to know how best to respond to them. Without relocation, without living among the people, without actually becoming one of the people, it is impossible accurately to identify the needs as the people perceive them. Our best attempts to reach people from outside will patronise them . . .

'Jesus was equal to God, yet he gave that up and took the form of a servant. He took on the likeness of man. He came and lived among us. He was called Immanuel, "God with us". The incarnation is the ultimate relocation.'[4]

Perkins went on to say: 'Not only did God relocate among us by taking the form of a man, but when a fellowship of believers relocates into a community, Christ incarnate invades that community. Christ, as his body, as his church, comes to dwell there.'

This so challenged Nico and Ellen that they became the first Afrikaners to be given governmental permission to live in a black township, as we have already seen. In a world of 'cardboard cities', 'ethnic minorities' and 'inner city crisis', the church cannot remain silent. If we are to become instrumental in establishing the kingdom we must become people who know how to show mercy.

For some people that may mean relocation, but for all of us it will undoubtedly involve moving out of our cloistered mentality and taking the gospel to the nations. God, who is 'rich in mercy' (Ephesians 2:4), 'full of compassion and mercy' (James 5:11), desires to work through his body, the church.

The ultimate expression of mercy was the incarnation, God sending his Son in the likeness of sinful humanity. 'For this reason [Jesus] had to be made like his brothers in every way, in order that he might become a merciful and faithful high priest in service to God' (Hebrews 2:17).

God himself got right inside human skin. He relocated into this world as a man, to see things as we see them, to feel as we feel. He came to identify with men and women to set people free. He was not detached or isolated but showed mercy through the incarnation.

Showing mercy

As a young lad I loved to collect things. One of my favourite collections was a series of picture postcards. Each one had the photograph of a missionary on it with the printed words: 'Please pray for us.' When these servants of God were home on furlough, they would often stay in our home and thrill us with stories more exciting than any boys' annual. To my childlike mind, their lives seemed one big adventure story full of travel, danger – and the absence of washing facilities!

These people were willing to leave the comfort and security of the United Kingdom and set up home in some of the most appalling conditions in Africa. What made them go where no Western person had been before? What drove them to set up schools, hospitals and mission stations miles from civilisation? Was it to establish a piece of the British Commonwealth in darkest Africa? Was it to sow Victorian tradition and religious ethics into a foreign culture? I don't think so. Many of these ambassadors of the gospel desired only to empathise with another culture, to befriend people. They had no motive other than to show mercy – because they themselves had experienced mercy.

This desire to show mercy motivated a young housemaid who, though refused support from the missionary society, saved enough money for a one-way train ticket to China. Gladys Aylward became a naturalised Chinese citizen, empathising with the culture. She ate the strange local food and dressed as the Chinese. Why? In order to sympathise and show mercy to the people of China. William Booth, Albert Schweitzer, David Brainerd, George Müller and many more stand as classic examples of what it means to show mercy.

In more modern terms, Agnes Gonxha Bojaxhiu, or Mother Teresa as she is better known, is a shining example of what it means to exercise this angle of approach to life. Spurred on by an incident in which she found a dying woman whose feet had been half-eaten by rats and ants, she determined to set up a hospice for the terminally ill. She collected people off the streets, from garbage dumps and from under the bridges of Calcutta.

Mother Teresa describes the purpose of her venture in this way: 'We want to make them feel they are wanted . . . and that there are people who really love them, who really want them, at least for the few hours they may have to live . . . to know human and divine love.' On another occasion she said: 'The biggest disease today is not leprosy or tuberculosis, but . . . the feeling of being unwanted, uncared for and deserted by everybody.'[5]

Christianity has every right to be proud of its social reformers: William Wilberforce, who worked to abolish slavery; the Seventh Earl of Shaftesbury, who looked after chimney-sweep children; Robert Raikes, the father of Sunday schools; William Booth and his service to the poor, which started in the East End of London. Yet questions need to be asked. What has happened to the social conscience of the church today? Are we in danger of becoming so marginalised that we become unconcerned with the poverty and injustice that surrounds us? Am I willing to expose my life so as to hurt with those who are hurting? Have I become so self-sufficient that social issues have no part to play in my comfortable Christianity?

Where are those sons of the kingdom who will empathise with the poor and speak out against the issues of injustice and ill-treatment of minority groups? Is the social thermometer of the church showing a distinct lack of concern for those less fortunate than ourselves? Has the church become a middle-class ghetto, immunised against the effects of the real world? Have we become cocooned in our warm, air-conditioned environment?

May the Lord help us to present a gospel that is relevant, and empathise with the poor and oppressed.

Get out of jail free

'Blessed are the merciful, for they will be shown mercy' (Matthew 5:7). The reciprocal promise attached to this Beatitude is a theme found throughout Scripture. The New Testament insists that to be forgiven we must be willing to forgive. 'Judgement without mercy will be shown to anyone who has not been merciful' (James 2:13). Those who sow mercy will reap mercy.

The Lord's Prayer continues the theme when Jesus teaches us to say: 'Forgive us our debts, as we also have forgiven our debtors' (Matthew 6:12). Then again in Matthew 6:14–15: 'If you forgive men when they sin against you, your heavenly Father will also forgive you. But if you do not forgive men their sins, your Father will not forgive your sins.'

If you have ever played the world-famous board game Monopoly, the phrase 'Get out of jail free' will be familiar. At various points during the game you pick up a card entitled 'Get out of jail free'. If for some reason you happen to be sent to jail, the card allows you immediate release without missing a turn.

Like the Monopoly card, the attitude of 'showing mercy' is a key to spiritual freedom. Used correctly it keeps us free. If it is missing or is used wrongly, we risk spiritual, emotional and mental lock-up.

In the parable of the unmerciful servant (Matthew 18:21–35) we can see the implications of a unmerciful attitude. A wrong attitude is a matter of life and death. Because of this man's unmerciful attitude, his 'unforgiving spirit', he was 'handed ... over to the torturers until he should repay' (v34 NASB).

Once he had experienced mercy, he should have reciprocated with mercy. Instead, he refused to forgive the one who had offended him. This was contrary to the principles of Matthew 5:23–24. He therefore brought into play another law, the law of checks and balances. 'For with the measure you use, it will be measured to you' (Luke 6:38).

Thayer translates the Greek word *torturers* (Matthew 18:34) as 'to draw out truth by means of the rack'. The idea conveyed is that of a medieval torture in which the individual was strapped to a bench and, with a rope attached to his arms and legs, he was stretched until he confessed to the crime he had supposedly committed.

Roots of bitterness

A seed of offence sown into the ground of insecurity will soon take root. When we become offended by something a person has said or not said, done or not done, we allow the situation to fester and become blown out of all proportion.

If it is allowed to settle, a seed of offence will produce a 'bitter root ... to cause trouble' (Hebrews 12:15), and from this root the fruit of resentment grows. 'Resentment means to feel or to show displeasure at an act, person, remark or situation from a sense of injury or insult.'[6] Unresolved relationship issues can imprison a person in resentment, causing a whole host of troubles in his or her life. Resentment is symptomatic of a stubborn attitude and can produce fear (Jeremiah 4:14–19), complaining (Job 7:11) and negative talk (Ephesians 4:31).

The children of Israel were delivered from Egypt to preserve the purity of their beginnings. Yet soon they faced the bitter waters of Marah (Exodus 15:22–27). Getting Israel out of Egypt was relatively easy; getting the bitterness of Egypt out of Israel was much more difficult.

The early church, although brought to birth through the miraculous, had to confront the impure attitude of Ananias and Sapphira (Acts 5:1–11). In the same way the first priesthood faced its Nadab and Abihu, priests who 'offered strange fire before the Lord' (Numbers 3:3–4 NASB), and Cain and Abel faced their relational problem.

God will prepare for himself a pure church, 'a radiant church, without stain or wrinkle or any blemish, but holy and blameless' (Ephesians 5:27). It will be a redeemed community who, having experienced mercy, will show mercy to a dying world.

> *Lord, make me a channel of thy peace,*
> *that where there is hatred, I may bring love;*
> *that where there is wrong, I may bring*
> *the spirit of forgiveness;*
> *that where there is discord, I may bring harmony;*
> *that where there is error, I may bring truth;*
> *that where there is despair, I may bring hope;*
> *that where there is shadow, I may bring light;*
> *that where there is sadness, I may bring joy.*
> [A prayer reportedly written by St Francis of Assisi]

Notes

[1] Coretta Scott King, *The Words of Martin Luther King* (William Collins, 1983).

[2] *Independent* newspaper (Monday 21 May 1990).

[3] Martyn Lloyd-Jones, *Studies in the Sermon on the Mount* (IVP, 1971).

[4] Rebecca de Saintonge, *Outside the Gate*, (Hodder & Stoughton, 1989).

[5] Kathleen White, *Heroes of the Cross* (Marshall Pickering, 1985).

[6] Bob Mumford, *The Prison of Resentment* (Life Changers, 1977).

REDEMPTIVE ATTITUDE No 5

'Blessed are the merciful,
for they will be shown
mercy.'

'An ability to empathise
with other people, so that
we see how they see and
feel how they feel. In so
doing, our resolve is to
bring justice and righteousness
to bear.'

CHAPTER EIGHT

BACK TO THE IRONING BOARD

'Remind your people . . . not to speak evil of anyone, but to be peaceful and friendly, and always to show a gentle attitude towards everyone.'

Titus 3:1–2 [GOOD NEWS BIBLE]

'Nothing I discovered about the make-up of human beings contradicts in any way what I learn from the Hebrew prophets, and from Jesus and the lives of those he touched. Anything I can say as a result of my research into human behaviour is a mere footnote to those lives in the Old and New Testaments.' So wrote Robert Coles, described by *Time* magazine in a 1972 cover story as 'the most influential living psychiatrist in the US'.

Coles's five-volume series *Children of Crisis* ran to more than a million words, earning him a Pulitzer Prize in 1973. Later he was selected for the MacArthur Foundation 'Genius Award'. He spent twenty-five years researching his subject and travelling the world, cataloguing the effects of poverty and wealth on children.

In his moving account of Coles's conversion to Christianity, Philip Yancey tells how an interview with a disadvantaged, uneducated six-year-old black New Orleans slum dweller revolutionised his life.

Yancey writes: 'By the time the last of the *Children in Crisis* volumes had been published, Robert Coles had ended up not in a new place, but in a very old place. He had travelled thousands of miles, recorded miles of tape and written a million words, all of which pointed right back to the Sermon on the Mount. He had discovered that the poor are mysteriously blessed and that the rich live in peril. He had learned that what matters most comes not from without – the circumstances of life – but from within, inside the heart of an individual man or woman.'[1]

The Beatitudes were never intended to be a new set of commandments which the disciples had to strive to keep. Rather, they are a composite picture of Christian character. As we have seen, each attitude can be seen as a character trait self-evident in those who 'participate in the divine nature' (2 Peter 1:4), as natural to Christian life as roses to a rose bush.

Collectively, the Beatitudes express the source of personal well-being and blessing that is to be reflected in God's alternative society, the church. Here are eight redemptive attitudes, angles of approach to life seen in those who are seeking to advocate God's way. They exemplify those who sacrificially lay down their lives in order to seek out, raise up and bring back what was lost.

Now that Jesus has taught his followers four attitudes which relate to their relationship with God, he moves on to the theme of interpersonal relationship. Showing mercy and making peace are both to do with people's dealings with their fellow-humans. And central to the teaching on this subject is this key phrase: 'Blessed are the pure in heart, for they will see God' (Matthew 5:8).

What a strange place to bring up the subject of purity! Here we are, embroiled in the whole issue of relating with others, and Jesus serves notice of his intention to check our heart condition. Is there any real point in this, or is it just a case of bad timing? The sequence of events so far has been perfect. So is this Beatitude somehow different or out of place?

We are confronted with this issue of purity just after considering the various ingredients that are involved in showing mercy, and just before we embark on the subject of making peace. There is a reason for this. In fact, this Beatitude is the pivot to the whole theme of relating to other people.

The issue is one of motive. Where better to bring up this topic than right in the centre of the teaching on relating to others? 'Blessed are the pure in heart' is a kind of divine litmus test. If you like, it is a 'motive monitor' that checks our driving force in life. It is also a truth detector that exposes levels of anxiety around one fundamental question: 'What is the motive behind your showing mercy and making peace?'

Motives motivate

Motives propel us to action. The word 'motive' is derived from the same word as 'motor'. Just as a motor drives a vehicle, so motives are the propelling force behind the way we act and the direction we take. They motivate us either to act or not.

The 'pure heart' is a spiritual condition in which the individual acts from pure, godly motives. If, for instance, there is any measure of selfishness in our actions, our motives are classed as mixed. What to outsiders is done for Jesus can be tinted by a desire to be seen by others. In that case our motive is to gain remuneration or win people's favour. Although the action appears good, the motive is mixed and impure, thus disqualifying the deed.

A motive is usually described as a verb; our motive is 'to make money', 'to do God's will' or 'to be seen by people'. No matter what the motivation, it will always produce either overt or covert behaviour.

For instance, I may have a deep-seated motivation to become prominent among a certain group of people. I might therefore avoid mixing with those I consider unimportant. I might change my habits and lifestyle to create an acceptable image. My opinions might be altered to agree with those I want to impress. I might build relationships with the in-crowd, hatch schemes and plot how I could open doors otherwise closed to me. Yet all the time I could be unaware of what I am doing. Such overt behaviour patterns are driven by impure motives. Hence the reason for this motivational attitude: purity of heart.

'Blessed – happy, enviably fortunate, and spiritually prosperous [that is, possessing the happiness produced by experience of God's favour and especially conditioned by the revelation of his grace, regardless of their outward conditions] – are the pure in heart, for they shall see God!' (Matthew 5:8 Amplified Bible).

Checking from the neck up

On the subject of motives William Barclay wrote: 'It is very seldom indeed that we do even our finest actions from absolutely unmixed motives.'[2] In the light of Barclay's statement, the words of Jesus become very searching indeed.

They pose some pertinent questions: What is the driving force behind my evangelistic efforts towards the non-Christian? Am I befriending that neighbour as a means to an end? Do I see him as a project, potential pew fodder for the next outreach meeting? Have I taken on board the spirit of the age that sees people as 'contacts', 'numbers', 'statistics', 'stepping-stones' or 'faceless souls'?

The bland social malaise affecting society today is that people are no longer seen as unique individuals with personal thoughts, ambitions and needs. While the world community might find this *persona non grata* approach acceptable, the church has to guard itself against such a supercilious attitude.

Jesus treated the woman at the well with respect, even though her life was a mess. He saw her as someone who had personal thoughts, feelings, goals and unrealised ambitions – a unique individual whom God loved.

Jesus spoke of those who loved to be announced loudly and who performed their religious deeds in front of the crowd to earn acclamation and approval of people. He concluded simply: 'They have received their reward in full' (Matthew 6:5). What is the driving force behind your willingness to serve others? If it is to receive public recognition, you had better enjoy the accolades now, for there is no heavenly appreciation society that is going to condone such behaviour.

True servanthood flows from a pure source, a heart whose motives are clean and clear. Jesus said: 'I am among you as one who serves' (Luke 22:27). Every act of mercy and peace was born out of a pure motive. His actions were perfect, never for effect.

Paul wrote to the Ephesians on the issue of serving: 'Servants . . . be obedient to those who are your physical masters, having respect for them and eager concern to please them, in singleness of motive and with all your heart, as [service] to Christ [himself]. Not in the way of eyeservice – as if they were watching you – and only to please men; but as servants . . . of Christ, doing the will of God heartily and with your whole soul; rendering service readily with goodwill, as to the Lord and not to men' (Ephesians 6:5–7 Amplified Bible).

I remember on one occasion having to explain the meaning of Jesus' teaching on prayer to a godly Christian gentleman. He was unwilling to pray publicly and cited the following verse as a divine command not to pray out loud in public meetings: 'Be careful not to do your "acts of righteousness" before men' (Matthew 6:1).

Somehow he was missing the whole point. Jesus was speaking about mixed motives, not the rights and wrongs of praying publicly. The hypocrites gave money and prayed so as 'to be honoured by men' (Matthew 6:2). It was this kind of serving for effect that Jesus disqualified. His comments were directed to people wanting to receive the temporal adoration and appreciation of people, rather than an eternal reward of 'well done, thou good and faithful servant . . . have thou authority over . . . cities' (see Luke 19:11–27 KJV).

God does not recognise or reward any service that is for:

- Self-display.
- Prestige.

- Respectability.
- Superiority.
- Comfortable thoughts of self-righteousness.
- Building up credits.

These motives are hay and stubble – material that will not stand the test of divine scrutiny. As if to illustrate this principle the Tower of Babel, although appreciated by people, became unacceptable to God on an issue of motives. The people boasted of their motivational drive, saying: 'Come, let us build ourselves a city . . . so that we may make a name for ourselves and not be scattered' (Genesis 11:4).

We can all display magnificent *acts of mercy*. We pride ourselves on the walls of hostility we have demolished while negotiating peace. But if our motives are wrong, we automatically disqualify the action. God sees through us: 'The Lord does not look at the things man looks at. Man looks at the outward appearance, but the Lord looks at the heart' (1 Samuel 16:7).

Only a pure motive will procure the Father's eternal approval. The finest spiritual act done for self-appeasement or public applause is judged hypocritical and therefore unfit. Jesus is teaching his disciples in Matthew 5 to check their motives, for right motives come from a pure heart.

Motives can be *selfish*. Our finest actions can be tarnished by this 'me, my and mine' generation. If what we say and do issues from an independent, self-centred attitude which characterises so much of this present society, it becomes unacceptable as service pleasing to the Master.

Motives can also be *social*. What at face value appears to be an act of kindness to the unregenerate person, a means to promote God's kingdom, is actually borne out of a friendship with the world which, according to James, is hatred towards God (James 4:4–10).

True motives must be *spiritual*. This word is not used in a religious sense; we are talking here about actions borne out of an interaction of the Holy Spirit with my spirit. As a result, I can show God's mercy and bring true peace without any ulterior motive.

A pure heart

The Greek word for pure is *katharos*, which means 'clean'. It has the idea of something that is 'free from mixture or anything that soils, adulterates or corrupts'. It is like unalloyed gold, unmixed wine or unadulterated milk. It was a word used for purging an army of cowards, dissidents and inefficient soldiers, to produce a first-class fighting force.

During the days of communist clamp-down in the Soviet Union, Christians had to meet in secret for fear of imprisonment. One such group, singing and worshipping God in a cabin far away from any town or city, was suddenly interrupted by a heavy banging on the door. All at once it burst open to reveal a Russian soldier. Fearful for their lives, the people waited to see what would happen next.

'Anyone who isn't willing to give his life for Jesus Christ get outside,' he shouted.

A few people immediately left the room. When they had gone the soldier stepped inside and sat down with the remaining Christians as if to enjoy their company. To their look of sheer amazement, he quietly said: 'I'm a born-again believer. I only want to share fellowship with people who are true Christians, and who are willing to lay down their lives for the kingdom!'

To purify means to purge an army of cowards.

Although *katharos* meant clean, it soon became a word that took on the idea of being 'free from what is false or insincere'. It was used to describe corn that had to be processed in order to separate the chaff from the pure wheat.

J B Phillips translates this Beatitude: 'Happy are the utterly sincere, for they will see God!' And Barclay puts it: 'Blessed is the man whose motives are always entirely unmixed, for that man shall see God.'[3]

Here Jesus is penetrating the very depths of our being. He is concerned with the heart, for that is the source of all acts of kindness. 'Keep thy heart with all diligence; for out of it are the issues of life' (Proverbs 4:23 KJV). The heart is the centre or seat of a person's moral affection, the fulcrum of all feelings, the core of one's character. The Hebrew word translated 'heart' literally means 'centre'. It is the mainspring of our words and actions (see Romans 10:10; Matthew 12:34; 15:19; 22:37; John 14:1), the fountain head from which everything else flows. 'Above all else, guard your heart, for it is the wellspring of life' (Proverbs 4:23).

It is crucial therefore that we guard from all impurities the 'wellspring' of our actions. This will avoid any corruption or mixed motive to foul the source of our outward behaviour. We could paraphrase this Beatitude: 'Blessed is the man whose heart [his core and centre] is free from all impurities and anything that corrupts.'

Without folds

There is another way of explaining the phrase 'purity of heart'. As we have seen, it means first and foremost to be clean, free from impurities. But a second meaning to is 'an undivided heart' or, more literally, 'a heart without folds'.

When the Bible speaks of being pure it is meaning sincerity, being transparent and crystal clear. It is the complete opposite to being hypocritical. The hypocrite is like an actor wearing a mask, pretending to be what he or she is not. It is like the person we refer to as 'two-faced'. What is seen is not the true person, but a pretence, an act, a show.

Purity of heart in many ways corresponds with the term 'singleness of eye', which Jesus uses later in his Sermon on the Mount (see Matthew 6:19–25 KJV). Again it means 'without folds'; it is open, with nothing hidden. Purity of heart is sincerity; it is single-minded or single-eyed devotion.

One of the best definitions of purity is given in Psalm 86:11: 'Give me an undivided heart, that I may fear your name.' The trouble with us is our divided heart. One part wants to know and worship God and to please him and the other part wants something else. The pure heart is the heart that is no longer divided. That was the Psalmist's dilemma concerning his heart. 'Make it one,' he seems to say, 'make it single, take out the pleats and the folds, let it be whole, let it be one, let it be sincere, let it be entirely free from any hypocrisy.'[4]

To be truly 'pure in heart' is to have a singleness of purpose, a resolve to serve one Master, not to act from a hypocritical attitude. If, as Dr Barclay reckoned, many of our finest actions are from impure motives, we need to go back to the ironing board to allow the Holy Spirit to straighten us out; we need to allow him to remove the creases from the very fabric of our heart that is otherwise clean.

This attitude, more than any other, will determine where we store our treasure and how we serve others (see Matthew 6:19–24). It is what the Old Testament means when it talks about being wholehearted (NASB: Jeremiah 24:7; Psalm 119:2,10; Deuteronomy 4:29; 1 Kings 11:4). If like King David we want to serve God's purposes in our generation (Acts 13:36), we must serve God and other people with a whole heart. We need to be like David, 'a man after [God's] own heart' (1 Samuel 13:14).

Many Christians divide their lives into secular and sacred compartments. It is far better to see our whole life as an extension of kingdom rule.

I might take a piece of paper, hold it up for inspection and say: 'Look how clean this is.' But if you were to look at it closely you would see that, although the paper is clean of any visible marks, it is folded in two. At first you see only a half. When the sheet of paper is opened out, you see it in its entirety. There is a crease, a fold in the centre of the page. It may be clean, but it is not clear. Our finest actions may appear at first to be spotless, but a close inspection of the underlying motives reveals that they are mixed.

Purity of heart means that even under the microscopic inspection of God's all-seeing eye, our actions are rooted in a heart that is unbiased, without prejudice. For some of us, that kind of scrutiny might mean going back to God in order to get things ironed out. Perhaps that majestic deed done in the name of the Lord had an ulterior motive. Or that act of kindness seemingly done with a clear conscience had some repayment clause in the small print.

How often are our good deeds done with mixed motives, a sense of reservation, bias or prejudice? Paul wrote to the Colossians: 'Servants, obey in all things your masters according to the flesh, not with eye-service, as men-pleasers; but in singleness [sincerity] of heart, fearing God' (Colossians 3:22 RAV; see also Ephesians 6:5–6). According to Robert Young, the Greek word *haplotes*, translated 'singleness', literally means: 'Freedom from duplicity.'[6]

Singleness or sincerity of heart means 'to be open, without ulterior motive, unambiguous (having double meaning), wholehearted, free from pretence'. It is the way in which Paul said he had conducted himself in the world and his relationship with God's people: 'With devout and pure motives and godly sincerity' (2 Corinthians 1:12 Amplified Bible).

David willingly gave of himself and his wealth to build the temple. He said: 'I know, my God, that you test the heart and are pleased with integrity. All these things have I given willingly and with honest intent' (1 Chronicles 29:17).

Integrity

Sex scandals, unfaithfulness, perjury, fraud, misappropriation of company funds, welshing on a deal – these are all symptomatic of a culture that lacks integrity. The ability to keep our promises is fundamental to our survival. It is an issue of life and death.

Permanently engraved on the minds of many American people is the horrific explosion of the Challenger space shuttle. As Christa McAuliffe prepared to be the first citizen to fly aboard a space-shuttle mission, she had no idea that her life was precariously balanced on the scales of human integrity. That cold January morning was a great concern to the engineers and designers alike. Would the booster seals work in such low temperatures? The engineers said, 'No.' Those with greater influence said, 'Yes.'

At 11:39 am on 28 January 1986, just seventy-three seconds into the flight, Challenger burst into a fireball of smoke, flame and twisted metal.

In his book *Integrity*, Ted Engstrom wrote of this incident: 'Power overruled reason. Integrity was the victim. After seventy seconds of flight, a faulty booster rocket ignited millions of gallons of rocket fuel into a blinding explosion. Debris rained on the Florida waters for a solid hour. At first we believed that Christa and the other six crew members perished instantly at the moment of explosion. Upon examination of the cabin remains, we have since learned they may have endured almost three and a half minutes of terrifying freefall before smashing into the Atlantic Ocean at 200 miles per hour. I only wish these words about the urgent need for integrity could carry that same force of impact.'[7]

Over the months that followed, a federal investigation unearthed evidence to show that the disaster could have been avoided. NASA had been warned four years earlier that the O-ring booster seals were unreliable. Yet top officials insisted that the programme continue, despite last-minute pleas to postpone the launch.

'Before the first shuttle was launched,' wrote Ed Magnuson in *Time* magazine, 'the agency had known of the fatal seal problem but had buried it under a blizzard of paper while permitting schedule-conscious managers to keep the orbiters flying.'[8] Expediency may have won, but integrity was lost.

Integrity means simply doing what we said we would! The Hebrew word *tom* is translated 'integrity' in the Old Testament. Its plural form is the word *thummim*. The same word was used for a part of the High Priest's ceremonial accoutrements used in the Tabernacle of Moses, the Tent of God's dwelling during Israel's wilderness wanderings.

'Whenever Aaron enters the Holy Place, he will bear the names of the sons of Israel over his heart on the breastpiece of decision as a continuing memorial before the Lord. Also put the Urim and the Thummim in the breastpiece, so they may be over Aaron's heart whenever he enters the presence of the Lord. Thus Aaron will always bear the means of making decisions for the Israelites over his heart before the Lord' (Exodus 28:29–30).

Urim means 'lights' and *Thummim* means 'perfection'. The *Urim* and the *Thummim* are steeped in mystery and have been the subject of much debate. While scholars continue to argue over what they were, two things are certain: Aaron was to keep them near to his heart, and they were crucial for making decisions.

In our desire to show mercy and make peace, we need to be protected by 'the breastplate of righteousness' (Ephesians 6:14). This will ensure that our external deeds issue from a pure heart, an inner source that is both clean and clear of any ulterior or mixed motives.

The weights and measures man

As a young lad being brought up in a hardware store, I became adept at using the shop's old-fashioned weights and scales. I had hours of enjoyment as I measured and weighed out nails of all shapes and sizes as well as putty by the pound.

The brass weights were my favourite. I soon discovered a hole at the base of each weight into which molten lead had been poured. The picture of a crown had been impressed on the lead. This set the exact weight against the correct standard. When I tried to dig out the lead with my penknife my dad gave me a swift clip around the ear.

As the years passed, I came to understand the significance of the annual visit of a government inspector known simply as 'the weights and measures man'. As he carefully checked each measure and weight against his perfect standard set by the Crown, we awaited his verdict. Anyone tampering with a set standard was treated very severely by the courts.

God's standards are no different. It is against his standards that all actions and behaviour are measured. Any tampering with the standard disqualifies our finest actions. Under divine scrutiny it should be possible to use the same words about our lives that were used of Nathanael: 'Here is an Israelite indeed . . . in whom there is no guile nor deceit nor falsehood nor duplicity!' (John 1:47 Amplified Bible).

We must be aware of double standards. For example, if I demand that the children appear instantly when they are called to dinner, while I can be ten minutes late, that is a double standard and a bad example. Or I might use verbal manipulation – arranging facts or putting an emphasis on one aspect so as to twist the truth and get the response I am after. Such things flow from an insincere heart.

True, these aspects were raised under the heading of righteousness, but now the theory must come into practice. 'Blessed

– happy, enviably fortunate, and spiritually prosperous . . . are the pure in heart, for they shall see God!' (Matthew 5:8 Amplified Bible). Our prayer needs to be: 'Teach me your way, O Lord, and I will walk in your truth; give me an undivided heart, that I may fear your name' (Psalm 86:11).

Bob Mumford writes: 'Pure in heart? This does not have to do with a heart without sin – though there will be a turning from all known sin. The deeper meaning is "one without guile". Jesus described one of his disciples, Nathanael, as being a man without guile (see John 1:47).

'Guile is deceit-pretence. It is easy to "play games" in an attempt to enter the kingdom. But God distinguishes the real from the sham. A façade of "wouldest-shouldest-canst" will not impress the Father. He wants us to come and talk to him according to the intents of our hearts – not according to ritual or prescribed traditions of men. If there is a question or doubt – get it out into the open. Then he can reveal himself to you and meet your needs. You will see God and be blessed.'[9]

The law of vision

'Blessed are the pure in heart, for they will see God.' If my action is motivated from a singleness of heart (without mixture, undivided), it will result in a singleness of eye, an ability to see God's purposes in and through conflicting situations (see Matthew 6:21). While redemption removes the mist of spiritual ignorance (2 Corinthians 4:3–12), only a purity of heart will facilitate a clarity of vision.

James throws some light on this attitude when he says: 'Purify your hearts, you double-minded' (James 4:8). Where there is mixture, purification has to take place. Remember, 'a double-minded man (is) unstable in all he does' (James 1:8). The pure heart is an 'undivided heart' and the Psalmist's prayer is valid here: 'Teach me your way, O Lord, and I will walk in your truth; give me an undivided heart, that I may fear your name. I will praise you, O Lord my God, with all my heart' (Psalm 86:11–12). This, as we have already seen, literally means 'without folds' – not having mixed motives or double standards, but pure and transparent, with nothing hidden.

We only see what we are able to see. For example, most of us see clusters of lights in the night sky, yet a knowledgeable person calls each star by name, and transatlantic yachtsmen steer their vessels by them. Most of us see clumps of unsightly weeds under the hedgerow, but the botanist sees precious plants that can all be named. Some people see a room full of so-called junk, but the historian sees architectural artefacts.

In a similar way, eight of the Old Testament spies saw giants, the other two saw God. Elisha's servant saw the enemy; Elisha saw the armies of God. Moses 'saw' the one who is invisible (Hebrews 11:27). What we have here is what I call 'The Law of Vision'.

If we have a pure heart our motives will also be pure. We are more likely to see God's purpose in things. The pure see with God's eyes. Like Joshua and Caleb, they see God driving out the unlawful inhabitants and giving them the land. The others merely see giants and high walls (Numbers 13:30–14:9). Joshua and Caleb saw God, not just the natural circumstances. As a result, God fulfilled his promises: 'Because my servant Caleb has a different spirit and follows me wholeheartedly, I will bring him into the land he went to, and his descendants will inherit it' (Numbers 14:24).

Vision is vital

The inability to see is restrictive. 'Where there is no vision, the people perish' (Proverbs 29:18 KJV). The Hebrew word translated 'perish' also means 'disintegrate' or 'be unrestrained'. The loss of personal vision not only restrains us but removes our impetus to press forward. Without an ultimate goal in life we are liable to go off at many different tangents.

Vision *monitors*; it keeps us going in a prescribed direction. A vision will help us judge the rights and wrongs of involving ourselves in particular activities. Abraham left Ur of the Chaldees and became a stranger in a foreign country because he was 'looking forward to the city with foundations, whose architect and builder is God' (Hebrews 11:10). Moses turned his back on a privileged lifestyle and joined himself to his own people 'because he saw him who is invisible' (Hebrews 11:27). Vision is focus; it gives perspective in a situation or circumstance.

Joseph monitored his own life according to a vision he received as a teenager. His success, even in adverse circumstances, was due in no small part to his dream. At the close of his life he gave strict instructions concerning his mortal remains: the children of Israel were to carry his bones for 40 years until they entered the promised land. Why? Because he had caught a vision of God's purposes and it had become his ultimate goal.

Vision *motivates*; it is the driving force that keeps us pressing on even in desperate circumstances. Abraham pursued his destiny in life because he had caught a glimpse of something eternal. 'By faith Abraham, when called to go to a place he would later receive as his inheritance, obeyed and went . . . he made his home in the promised land like a stranger in a foreign country; he lived in tents, as did Isaac and Jacob, who were heirs with him of the same promise. For he was looking forward to the city with foundations, whose architect and builder is God' (Hebrews 11:8–10).

In the late 1960s American Aerospace noted how the principle of vision and motivation worked among its employees. Faced with the challenge of putting a man on the moon, the company saw average employees demonstrating extraordinary levels of performance. Yet once that mission was achieved, performance slumped. Vision causes ordinary people to do extraordinary things.

They will see God

If the principle is clear and the practice follows, the promise will ensue that 'they shall see God!' (Matthew 5:8 Amplified Bible). An undivided heart does not have mixed motives or double standards, but is pure and transparent with nothing hidden. Such a heart will see God in all situations. Some of these are listed below, beginning with the difficult ones.

'We can be full of joy here and now even in our trials and troubles. These very things will give us patient endurance; this in turn will develop a mature character, and a character of this sort produces a steady hope, a hope that will never disappoint us' (Romans 5:3–5 J B Phillips).

Corrie ten Boom beautifully illustrates this point. She, together with thousands of other prisoners, was transferred to a new prisoner-of-war camp at Ravensbrück in Germany. They were housed in harrowing conditions including wooden bunks, straw mattresses and fouled blankets. But that was not all. Once they had managed to climb on to the second level of a three-tier bunk, they found that their beds were infested with fleas!

Corrie seemed unperturbed by the situation. Turning to her sister Betsie, she excitedly related a way in which they could see God in this situation. The fleas would become the means of keeping the prison guards at bay. As a result, both ladies began to give thanks. The circumstances hadn't changed, but from a pure heart they saw God through the overcast and stormy environment of the concentration camp.

Caleb, as we have already observed, showed 'a different attitude' from the rest of the spies, even when faced by considerable opposition. He and Joshua saw the same opposing factors the ten other spies saw, but unlike the others they also saw God. The ten saw the giants in the land and said: 'We seemed like grasshoppers in our eyes, and we looked the same to them' (Numbers 13:33).

Joshua and Caleb, on the other hand, said: 'Do not be afraid of the people of the land, because we will swallow them up. Their protection is gone, but the Lord is with us. Do not be afraid of them' (Numbers 14:9). Caleb, with a different attitude, could see God in the midst of great opposition.

As a teenager I remember hearing the story of a Christian man living in Kenya, East Africa, during the Mau Mau uprisings. One evening after a prayer meeting he returned to his village home with a friend and was met by the sight of a community wrecked by rebel forces on the rampage. He rushed into his own home and found that his wife and children had all been killed.

He stepped outside to tell his friend what had happened. With tears streaming down his cheeks, he cried: 'The Lord gave and the Lord has taken away; may the name of the Lord be praised' (Job 1:21). In the midst of the trauma and heartache of this awful scene, this man was able to see God, as Job had done. 'My ears had heard of you but now my eyes have seen you' (Job 42:5).

We, too, will be able to see God in the midst of our opportunities. In serving others from pure motives, the righteous see God in their service. 'The righteous will answer him, "Lord, when did we see you hungry and feed you, or thirsty and give you something to drink? When did we see you a stranger and invite you in, or needing clothes and clothe you? When did we see you sick or in prison and go to visit you?" The King will reply, "I tell you the truth, whatever you did for one of the least of these brothers of mine, you did for me"' (Matthew 25:37–40).

Here then we have an angle of approach which will enable us

to see God in the darkest of circumstances. Mixed motives see the trouble and miss God; a purity of heart precipitates a greater revelation of God's presence and purpose in my life.

Back to the ironing board

This attitude spotlights every action that precedes or follows it. It asks the question: 'What are my motives for showing mercy and making peace? Are they mixed or sincere?' So often we put on the garments of servanthood, only to realise that our motives are not altogether pure.

We need to allow God to remove the creases. It is time to go back to the ironing board. Our prayer must be: 'Father, help us to be spurred into action by motives which are pure.'

Paul said to Timothy, his son in the faith: 'Pursue righteousness, faith, love and peace . . . out of a pure heart' (2 Timothy 2:22). Having given Timothy some direction regarding his pastoral work in the town of Ephesus, Paul said: 'The goal of this command is love, which comes from a pure heart and a good conscience and a sincere faith' (1 Timothy 1:5).

Notes

[1] Philip Yancey, *Christianity Today* magazine (February 1987).
[2] William Barclay, *The Daily Study Bible Series* (The Westminster Press, 1975).
[3] Barclay, op., cit.
[4] Martyn Lloyd-Jones, *Studies in the Sermon on the Mount* (IVP, 1971).
[5] Lloyd-Jones, op., cit.
[6] Robert Young, *Analytical Concordance* (Lutterworth, 1967).
[7] Ted W Engstrom, *Integrity* (Word, 1987).
[8] *Time* (6 September 1986).
[9] Bob Mumford, *The King and You* (Revell, 1974).

REDEMPTIVE ATTITUDE No 6

'Blessed are the pure in heart,
for they will see God.'

'An angle of approach to life
whereby we seek to show
mercy and make peace
without any ulterior motive,
other than to promote God's
purpose in the lives
of others.'

CHAPTER NINE

BRIDGE OVER TROUBLED WATERS

'Guard your attitude, so that it may be governed by my Spirit, says the Lord.'

Malachi 2:16 [PARAPHRASED]

Snuggling down into his warm, comfortable bed Pastor Cho began to relax his mind from the rigours of a busy day. He let his mind go, forgetting the numerous challenges he had already faced, the people he must contact tomorrow and the correspondence awaiting a response. All these began to fade as he slipped slowly into a deep sleep.

Suddenly, the silence was shattered by the unmistakable ring of the telephone. In a half-conscious state he began fumbling for the phone as he tried to compose his thoughts.

'Hello.'

'Pastor, do you know me?' enquired the voice on the other end of the phone.

Pastor Cho recognised one of his church members. 'Of course I know you. I married you and your wife.'

'I've tried for two years, but our marriage isn't working,' replied the caller. 'Tonight we've had a big argument and decided to separate. We've divided all our money and we're ready to go our separate ways. There's just one thing we'd like you to do.'

'What's that?' inquired the pastor, who by now was fully awake.

'We were married with your blessing, so we'd like you to bless our divorce.'

'Can't it wait till tomorrow? It's cold and I'm already in bed.'

'No, tomorrow's too late. We've decided to part. We don't need a counsellor. It's too late for that – it's all over between us. We just simply want you to give your blessing on the divorce.'

Rising wearily from his bed, Pastor Paul Yonggi Cho of Seoul, Korea, began to call on God for help and guidance. As he prayed, the Holy Spirit envisioned him with a possible marital reconciliation and reunion. With the vision came the faith to believe for a miracle and a redemptive attitude to bring back what was lost.

As he arrived at the couple's luxurious apartment that night, it was very apparent that they lacked nothing in terms of financial wealth. But the atmosphere was as icy inside as it was out. The hatred that existed between them was almost tangible.

Dr Cho describes what happened then: 'As I came in I found the man sitting in the living room and the wife in the bedroom. As soon as I walked into the living room the man began to speak derogatorily about his wife. His wife then rushed into the room saying, "Don't listen to him! Listen to me!" Then she also began to speak out against her husband.

'I would listen to the husband, and everything that he said seemed to be right. Then I would listen to the wife, and everything that she said seemed to be right; each was right in his own opinion. Both were right, and I was sandwiched between.

'Both said they were completely finished in their marriage. "Don't pray for us," they kept repeating. "Just pray for our divorce."

'But I had already overruled this . . . Being confident, I took the hand of the husband and the hand of the wife, and I said, "In the name of Jesus Christ, I command Satan to loose his hold of hatred on this couple. And in this moment, in the mighty name of Jesus Christ I command that these two be melted together. Let them be tender and rejoined."

'Suddenly I felt a warm drop fall on my hand, and when I looked at the man he was crying, and his tears were falling down . . . When I looked at the eyes of the wife I could see that her eyes were watering also. So I drew their hands together and said, "What the Lord has joined, let no man or circumstances divide."'

When asked later what happened on that eventful evening, the wife replied, 'Well, we don't know . . . But when you said those words and gave such strong commands, we felt something break down in our hearts. It was as if a wall had been destroyed, and we were shaken . . . After you left, we spent the entire night unpacking all our things . . . Now we love each other even more than before.'[1]

What was Dr Cho doing? Using a redemptive angle of approach to this couple, he took on the role and responsibility of a peacemaker: 'Blessed – enjoying enviable happiness, spiritually prosperous [that is, with life-joy and satisfaction in God's favour and salvation, regardless of their outward conditions] – are the makers and maintainers of peace, for they shall be called the sons of God!' (Matthew 5:9 Amplified Bible).

Although the peacemaker is mentioned only twice in the whole of the New Testament (Matthew 5:9; James 3:18), it is nevertheless an important role. There is no reason to believe that the role of the peacemaker is obsolete. This is despite a degenerating society in turmoil, national and international conflict on every hand, the breakdown of the nuclear family, and religious, ethnic and sectarian division.

The peacemaker

Never before in the field of human conflict has there been such a need for the emergence of godly peacemakers. We need men and women who, like Pastor Cho, will act as a bridge over troubled waters. We need divine go-betweens, people who actively involve themselves in the process of bringing God's peace into a divided society.

Such a ministry does not simply advocate the promotion of

human happiness and personal well-being. Nor does it merely take a passive stance and point others to a place where they might find peace with God. The role of the peacemaker and peacekeeper is the active involvement of a third person. Such a person steps between contending parties to restore God's peace where conflict has left turmoil in its wake. Peacemaking is a costly mission in terms of time, effort and emotional strain. And it calls for a painful involvement in the scrummage of life.

Although healthy interpersonal relationships are vital to people's existence, sin has eroded relational living on three levels. It ruined the relationship first between people and God, second between individuals and finally between people and their neighbours. Through redemption, God has reversed the process and paved a way by which relationships can be mended. In Christ we are able to enter into and enjoy a right relationship with God. We can also accept, appreciate and approve of ourselves.

This in turn enables us to love our neighbours as we love ourselves. In and through the redemptive merits of the cross, men and women can know personally not only 'the God of peace' but also 'the peace of God'. In this way, people come to peace with themselves and therefore adequately equipped to be employed as 'peacemakers'.

The opposite to peacemaking is troublemaking. Some people always seem to become 'the eye of the hurricane' wherever they go. They either cause an argument or become part of it. They are quarrelsome, touchy, sensitive and defensive – bona fide 'troublemakers'. Regarding such people the Bible warns us to be on our guard, to watch, mark, correct and if necessary avoid such people (Romans 16:17; Titus 3:10; 1 Thessalonians 5:13, 15).

At the other end of the spectrum there are those who hate conflict and will avoid confrontation at all cost. Their motto is 'anything for a quiet life' and their approach is one of appeasement, compromise, evading the issue or pacifying. They bite their tongue rather than say what they really think. These are the characteristics of the person who seeks peace at any price, someone who might be termed a 'trucemaker'.

In Matthew 5:9 Jesus is neither condoning the troublemaker nor commending the trucemaker. He is calling for peacemakers – godly individuals who see their role as bridge-builders, go-betweens, middlemen and mediators. They are people who are crucial for making and keeping peace, both in and out of the body of Christ.

Dr John Kennedy wrote of a unique sense of togetherness enjoyed by a group of Christians meeting in Ross-shire, Scotland, towards the end of the eighteenth century: 'Their enemies did call them "bigots", "enthusiasts", and "fanatics", but they did not dare to say they were not Christians. They were compelled to acknowledge that they were "sincere", "upright", and "well-meaning", though "very straitlaced" and "righteous overmuch". And they loved one another.

'Sometimes differences would arise, but they were felt by them all as a family affliction would be felt. In such cases a peacemaker would be always found. Sometimes his task would be made an easy one.

'One of them, hearing of a quarrel between two of his brethren, set off at once to make peace. Meeting one of the offenders, he asked, "Is it true that you and James have quarrelled?" "Oh, yes; alas! it is quite true," was the reply; "but James is not to be blamed – the fault is all mine." "If I find James," he remarked, "in the same state of mind, I expect very soon to see you at one again."

'On reaching the other, he said. "I am sorry to hear that you have quarrelled with John." "Oh, yes," he replied, "but it was my hasty temper that did all the mischief." "Come with me, then," the peacemaker said, "and confess your fault to your brother." He at once agreed to accompany him; and, no sooner did the separated brethren meet, than they embraced each other, mutually forgave and were forgiven, and continued ever after "in the bond of peace".'[2]

Peacemakers have a creative ability to bring a calming influence on others. This ability is a direct result of the godly manner in which they conduct their own lives. They are not passive bystanders but aggressive arbiters laying their lives on the line to bring a righteous solution. Bob Mumford wrote of those who portray this redemptive attitude in a godly manner: 'It isn't necessarily a matter of words, though these may be involved at times. It is rather, when you walk into a situation where sparks are flying and tempers are short – does the situation get better or worse?'[3]

The peace of God

The basic ingredient of these industrious individuals is 'peace'. While the peacemaker is the channel, the contents of his/her role is peace. In secular terms, peace is often viewed simply as 'the cessation of war or freedom from conflict'. This somewhat negative notion of peace is a poor cousin to the Hebrew concept of peace.

Peace is a godly virtue. An integral part of him whose name is 'the God of peace' (Romans 15:33;16:20; Philippians 4:9). The biblical view of peace is more than a mere absence of conflict. God's peace in both the Old and New Testaments is never simply a negative state – the absence of trouble. Rather, it is a positive, full-orbed word containing great wealth, health and general well-being. It is a peace 'not . . . as the world gives' (John 14:27).

The Hebrew word *shalom* carries the thought of a pervading inner tranquillity. God's peace reaches every part of us. It involves the total well-being of an individual, including good health and prosperity, to the extent that he or she is living a life of fullness and contentment. The recipient of God's peace lacks no good thing and is complete physically, materially and emotionally.

Health

When he was reunited with his brothers, Joseph demonstrated a redemptive attitude to those who had so cruelly mistreated him. He asked first after their health (Genesis 43:27). He then asked: 'How is your aged father?' In both instances he used the word or phrase translated from the Hebrew *shalom*. This Jewish greeting, *shalom*, which is Hebrew for 'peace', conveys the meaning of harmony, prosperity and all-round, full-orbed, positive blessing.

Joseph was himself at peace. He could therefore take up an angle of approach to life that was redemptive. Consumed with a passion for God's purpose and constrained by love, Joseph sought to seek out, raise up and bring back what was lost – harmonious family relationships.

Wealth

'The Lord be magnified, who delights in the prosperity of his servant' (Psalm 35:27 NASB). The word translated here as 'prosperity' is *shalom*. The prophet Isaiah goes on to endorse this when he declares God's will for his people: 'The Lord says: "I will extend peace to her like a river, and the wealth of nations like a flooding stream"' (Isaiah 66:12). God's peace is intimately associated with the financial well-being of God's people.

Welfare

Jeremiah suffered much in the course of his prophetic ministry, having been thrown into dungeons and a disused well. The trouble was, officials to King Zedekiah didn't believe his words were conducive to the people's general well-being. 'This man is not seeking the good of these people but their ruin,' they retorted (Jeremiah 38:4). The word 'good' (or *shalom*) used here has by implication the thought of welfare and well-being.

There are a number of other instances where *shalom* conveys the same message. Boaz acknowledges Ruth's loyalty to her mother-in-law and blesses her, saying: 'May the Lord reward your work, and your wages be full from the Lord, the God of Israel, under whose wings you have come to seek refuge' (Ruth 2:12 NASB). In view of what Ruth has done, Boaz calls for her reward to be full, complete and perfect.

It is the peacemaker's role and responsibility to involve himself/herself actively in the family, church and nation. The peacemaker mediates, arbitrates, reconciles, negotiates and intercedes to bring godly peace where there is no peace. These godly characteristics distinguish those who are citizens of God's kingdom, those who claim the birthrights of God's family, who reckon themselves 'sons of God'.

Peacemaking personified

The one whose birth was announced by those angelic words 'peace on earth' was himself 'the Prince of Peace'. Jesus, the peacemaker personified, entered the arena of cultural, social, religious and political division so as to still the storms of life.

He had a calming influence on those who followed him. He brought peace of mind to the person troubled with demons. He comforted those who were sick, bereaved and dying. He stilled the storm.

The religious leaders tried to embroil him in the spiritual arguments of the day. Jesus reconciled the seeming irreconcilable political difference between Jew and Roman with his reply: 'Give to Caesar what is Caesar's, and to God what is God's' (Luke 20:25). Jesus sought to make peace on the cross for all humankind by himself becoming the brunt of people's cruelty. Yet 'he uttered no threats, but kept entrusting himself to him who judges righteously' (1 Peter 2:23 NASB).

As the 'Prince of Peace' Jesus reconciled to 'himself all things, whether things on earth or things in heaven, by making peace through his blood, shed on the cross' (Colossians 1:20). Jesus, the peacemaker *par excellence*, broke down 'the barrier, the dividing wall of hostility' and made a way for everyone. We would be 'no longer foreigners and aliens' to the promises and purpose of God 'but fellow-citizens with God's people and members of God's household' (see Ephesians 2:14–22).

As citizens of God's kingdom and viceroys of his victory, we make peace by being the vehicle through whom the message of the gospel is spread. Our aim is to see men and women reconciled to God, making their peace with him and enjoying the blessings of sonship. As peacemakers our desire is to arbitrate, to reconcile, to stand as Moses did between the dead and the living and stop the plague (see Numbers 16:47–48). Our role is to act as an impartial third party who moves between two disputing or conflicting factions, just as Jesus the Son of God has already done in his work on the cross.

Peacemakers and peacekeepers are wise, understanding, 'pure . . . peaceable, gentle, reasonable, full of mercy and good fruits, unwavering, without hypocrisy', approachable, full of tolerance and kind actions, with no breath of favouritism or hint of hypocrisy (see James 3:17–18 NASB). Based on these words of James, a peacemaker is:

- Wise – Judges situations without human prejudice.
- Pure – Intervenes with right motives.
- Peaceable – Sets a good example.
- Gentle – Handles people sensitively.
- Reasonable – Fair.
- Full of mercy – Able to empathise and extend forgiveness.

- Unwavering – Sticks with decisions and sees people through difficult times.
- Without hypocrisy – Practises what he/she preaches at all times.

Above all, a peacemaker must be at peace himself. The peace-maker has tasted of the peace that results from being filled with the righteousness of Christ [see Diagram 1]. The peacemaker then desires to produce that same quality of peace in an environment where injustice and unrighteousness rule.

As a parent, the peacemaker mediates godly peace into family conflicts. As Christ's representative, the peacemaker brings peace, not just for the sake of peace and quiet, but to extend the rule of God in the home and see his blessing restored.

As a citizen, the peacemaker desires to become involved in issues of injustice and unrighteousness, which are often the result of Satan's covert activities in the community.

In line with the ethos of Christian peacemaking outlined in the Sermon on the Mount, the sons of God are called to take transforming initiatives to bring peace in the world. We are not merely to protest against an injustice. We are to involve ourselves in grace-filled initiatives that deliver people from being trapped in a vicious circle.

Some people would prefer to marginalise or monasticise Jesus' teachings as an impossible dream with unrealistic demands, totally impractical for today's society. Others see the Sermon on the Mount as the *locus classicus* for Christian peace-making.

On the other hand, some church organisations today are experimenting with alternative ways of rehabilitating criminals. They are thus demonstrating a true ministry of peacemaking through reconciliation. Their victim-offender reconciliation programme serves as a go-between. It brings victims and offenders together to pave the way for offenders to make some measure of restitution for the crime and seek reconciliation with the victim.

Through such initiatives, citizens of God's kingdom are being used to bring an end to social injustice, inner city deprivation and a social bias that gives preferential treatment on the basis of colour, class and creed.

No wonder creation cries: 'Bring on the sons of God!'! They alone can establish peace where there is no peace. The ministry of reconciliation – bringing two parties together for the purpose of renewing friendship after a period of estrangement – is an integral part of peacemaking.

Paul picks up this theme: 'God . . . reconciled us to himself through Christ and gave us the ministry of reconciliation: that God was reconciling the world to himself in Christ, not counting men's sins against them. And he has committed to us the ministry of reconciliation. We are therefore Christ's ambassadors' (2 Corinthians 5:18–20a; see also Colossians 1:21–22). Peacemakers seek to reconcile.

Mediation

A mediator acts as a go-between for two or more parties. This is something else in which Christ is involved. Paul reminded Timothy: 'There is one God and one mediator between God and men, the man Christ Jesus, who gave himself as a ransom for all men' (1 Timothy 2:5). The ransom here refers to the price paid to redeem a slave. Christ mediated between God and people in giving his life as the ransom price to free people from slavery to sin.

Similarly, the Old Testament priest was to mediate, to bear the needs and requirements of one to the other as appropriate. Jesus has this office as the great high priest (Hebrews 8:1,6). Peter reminds the church that they, too, form a royal priesthood (1 Peter 2:5). Peacemakers are mediators.

In among the tombstones of Eyam Parish Church, a quaint village set in the Derbyshire hills of England, is a simple stone monument to Thomas Stanley. The memorial reads: 'He stood between the dead and the living; and the plague was stayed. Numbers chapter 16, verse 48.'

The story of Thomas Stanley, formerly the rector of Eyam, is one of personal bravery and practical mediation. In September 1665 the village tailor, George Viccars, took delivery of some cloth which had just arrived from London. Now at last he would be able to finish his orders and satisfy his customers. But the clothes were never finished and Viccars would never again serve his community as their tailor. Within two days he became ill, stricken with a raging fever and strange swellings that developed into a rosy-red rash on his body. It was an illness from which he would not recover.

Between the Black Death of 1348 and the Great Plague of 1665 English life was smitten by bubonic plague. The plague was a bacterial disease spread through the black rat population. It was transmitted to humans through flea bites. Mr Viccar's box of cloth was infested with fleas and the village of Eyam would never be the same again.

Such was the terror that accompanied the plague that those in the village who could do so fled to friends and relatives. But Thomas Stanley, along with the rector of the day, William Mompesson, decided to stay and set up a system of quarantine.

They placed a circle of stones around the village to mark the boundary and got the villagers to agree to remain inside the circle. No one was allowed in and no one was allowed out. Courting couples who had been separated by the plague could be heard shouting their words of love to each other across the Derbyshire hills. Words of affection carried on the cool evening breeze of summer.

With the help of the Earl of Derbyshire, Stanley arranged for food and other necessities brought in from outside to be left at a fixed point. Payment for such items was left in running water to avoid any risk of infection.

The result of the plague in the village was terrifying. It took fifteen months for the epidemic to die out. From a population of 350, only eighty-three villagers survived. In just over a year, three-quarters of the inhabitants of Eyam had died. Had it not been for one man, the disease could have spread throughout the north of England. In the midst of turmoil, Stanley mediated peace. He stayed to the end to care for the sick and give aid to the suffering. He was truly a peacemaker.

In his death Thomas Stanley was remembered as one who 'stood between the dead and the living; and the plague was stayed'. In the middle of the conflict of death he laid his life on the line for others. He became expendable for the sake of bringing a resolve. His approach to life was redemptive, for his was the work of a peacemaker. 'Blessed – enjoying enviable happiness, spiritually prosperous [that is, with life-joy and satisfaction in God's favour and salvation, regardless of their outward conditions] – are the makers and maintainers of peace, for they shall be called the sons of God!' (Matthew 5:9 Amplified Bible).

Intercession

Perhaps the most important unseen work of a peacemaker is the ministry of intercession. As an intercessor, the peacemaker pleads the case of another before a higher authority who holds the power to improve that party's position.

During his earthly life, Jesus offered up prayers and petitions (Hebrews 5:7); now the Spirit continues that ministry in conjunction with Christ (Roman 8:26,34). Those who take on the role of peacemakers as 'sons of God' must learn how to intercede with the Holy Spirit. They must learn to plead the case of another before our heavenly Father, for he alone holds the power to bring peace to those caught up in life's conflicts. Paul teaches his son in the faith, Timothy, that a priority for peace-making is that 'first of all . . . requests, prayers, intercession and thanksgiving be made for everyone' (1 Timothy 2:1).

It must have been hard for my parents to handle a rebellious teenager who had been brought up in the ways of the Lord. I refused to listen to my parents' advice. My conflict of interest between the world and God's kingdom became all-consuming. The world began to take more and more spiritual territory, sapping my time, money and energy.

My mother, undeterred by my self-centred lifestyle and refusal to hear godly counsel, took the matter to God in prayer. She desperately wanted to bring peace to my warring spirit. As a result, intercession became her weapon of warfare. By God's grace and the efforts of a praying mother Christ's kingdom became triumphant. I came to heel and committed my life to God once more.

As I thumbed through my mother's Bible, given to me after her death, I began to read various marginal notes she had written during her times of prayer. Next to Psalm 138:8 KJV ('The Lord will perfect that which concerneth me'), she had written three simple words: 'Concerned for Christopher.' Praise God for peacemakers who take up the burden of intercession on behalf of others!

Arbitration

The arbitrator is a peacemaker appointed by two parties to settle a dispute between them. Job called for an arbiter who would assist him in pleading his innocence and the injustice of his plight (Job 9:32–33).

The arbiter's mission is to settle a dispute, to stop a conflict. In biblical terms cessation is the bottom line, while total well-being is the ultimate aim.

Based on the principles of Matthew 5:23–24 and 18:15–20, the process of arbitration involves first encouraging the conflicting parties to resolve their dispute on their own in private. If that doesn't work, a peacemaker is called for. If necessary, the parties may call on the church to arbitrate, both parties of the dispute agreeing to abide by the church's impartial judgement.

If we ignore this biblical process in resolving interpersonal conflict we run the risk of spiritual, mental and emotional lock-up. Like the unmerciful servant handed over to the torturers, the results of refusing the efforts of the peacemaker who seeks to bring godly wholeness and well-being can be devastating.

Peacemakers or peace-lovers?

There is a world of difference between a peace-lover and a peacemaker. Most people are peace-lovers. But because peace-making involves confrontation, conflict and tension, an essential ingredient of peacemaking is a willingness to make yourself vulnerable. Most people seem unwilling to get involved. They are not ready to experience what it means to be powerless, unprotected and, at times, the focus of vented frustrations.

Peacemakers allow others to speak their mind. They must be willing to listen and discuss. They must not be threatened when they hear ideas alien to their own. Above all, they must be free from any preconceived ideas. The aim is not peace at any price. There can be no true reconciliation, no genuine peace, without justice.

The peacemaker is a middleman. He/she listens to both parties in a dispute and encourages them to meet and discuss on the basis of what is righteous and just.

Biblically speaking there is a very strong link between peace and righteousness. The former is dependent on the presence of the latter. Isaiah says: 'The fruit of righteousness will be peace; the effect of righteousness will be quietness and confidence for ever' (Isaiah 32:17). From righteousness – the state and standing of being right before God – comes peace. Therefore, a life lived in a way acceptable to God will produce the fruit of peace. This will be evident initially by an inner quietness and strength, for 'those who walk uprightly enter into peace' (Isaiah 57:2).

The Psalmist further emphasises this bond when using that beautiful phrase 'righteousness and peace kiss each other' (Psalm 85:10). This marital imagery portrays a covenantal relationship between the two. Not only will a godly person live in a godly environment of peace with God, but that person will reproduce after his or her own kind. The natural product of a life in harmony with God is a progeny of peace – a peace which will permeate society.

It is not surprising, then, that Paul entreats Timothy to pursue 'righteousness, faith, love and peace . . . out of a pure heart' (2 Timothy 2:22). Righteousness becomes a prerequisite for acquiring and maintaining peace in a person's life. Apart from squaring the relationship with God at the outset, righteousness itself calls for a complete change in behaviour to bring it into line with the Word of truth. Peace cannot be divorced from a righteous lifestyle, for outside God peace cannot exist.

From a biblical perspective, conflicts within society demonstrate the absence of righteousness. If the precondition isn't met, the fruit isn't produced. Our prayer is: 'God, raise up Holy Spirit anointed peacemakers who, with godly wisdom, will bring an answer to the family, the church and the nation!'

'WANTED: Peacemakers! Urgently needed: people who are clean living, peace loving, courteous, considerate, open to reason, full of compassion, wholehearted, straightforward, impartial, free from doubts and insincerity. Peacemakers who sow in peace and raise a harvest of righteousness. Immediate start. Training provided. Excellent prospects. Apply within' (James 3:18 paraphrased).

The bond of peace

The peacemaker is motivated by an inner desire to see God's peace made and maintained in every sphere of human life. 'Make every effort to keep the unity of the Spirit through the bond of peace' (Ephesians 4:3), writes the Apostle Paul. We are eagerly to strive for and earnestly guard the binding power of peace, for it is peace that undergirds the work of God and society at large.

Like the ligaments which bind together the various parts of the human body, so the peace of God will avert a dislocation in the family, church and nation (Ephesians 4:16, where 'ligament' is the same word as 'bond'). Just as mortar acts as a bonding agent for a brick building, and as a cable holds a ship securely to its moorings, so peace holds together the very fabric of civilisation.

It is a fundamental role and responsibility of every child of the King to make and maintain God's peace. It is a redemptive attitude that seeks to restore what was lost. It is an angle of approach to everyday life that buys up opportunities to bring harmony, prosperity and full-orbed blessing to those in conflict.

Like Father, like Son!

When Scripture refers to someone as a 'son' of something or someone, it often means that the two have the same character or nature. So the term 'son of God' designates and marks out a God-likeness. Judas is called 'son of perdition' (John 17:12 NASB); Barnabas 'son of Encouragement' (Acts 4:36); and James and John 'sons of Thunder' (Mark 3:17).

In all these cases they lived up to their names by the way they behaved. Those who are called sons of God act like their heavenly Father, who establishes peace and seeks to be at peace with all men and women.

Although the ministry of the 'peacemaker' is mentioned only twice in the New Testament, it is not a minor one. Jesus himself recognised the fact that peace, when sown, would reap a harvest of righteousness or right-standing.

We bear the title 'sons of God'. This equates our ministry with that of Jesus himself. He embodied the role of a peacemaker and united two irreconcilable world groups – the Jews and the Gentiles: 'His purpose was to create in himself one new man out of the two, thus making peace, and in this one body to reconcile both of them to God through the cross, by which he put to death their hostility. He came and preached peace to you who were far away and peace to those who were near' (Ephesians 2:15–17).

By breaking down the dividing wall of the Mosaic law with its rules and regulations, Jesus made a way by which men and women could become parties to the covenant of promise.

The angels declared at the birth of Christ: 'Glory to God in the highest, and on earth peace among men with whom he is pleased' (Luke 2:14 NASB). This declaration can only be realised as God's redeemed community takes up the challenge of becoming peacemakers.

In a war-torn, degenerating society, the church has been given a mandate to make and maintain peace. 'Let us therefore make every effort to do what leads to peace and to mutual edification' (Romans 14:19). The world scene is set. Bring on the sons of God, for they alone are charged with the call to bring the much-needed peace.

A peacemaker is willing to stand in the midst of conflict and, from a standpoint of justice and righteousness, arbitrate, mediate, negotiate and intercede in order to reconcile two opposing factors.

According to Scripture Jesus will return not to a weak minority but to a strong, vibrant, influential body of committed Christians. The church will consist of believers who are exercising an impact on the world. The need for peacemakers and peacekeepers is therefore vital.

If an answer is to be found for the conflicts facing today's world, Christian peacemakers – who themselves are at peace – must re-emerge. Creation groans, waiting for the immediate as well as ultimate revelation of 'the sons of God' (Romans 8:19). Why? Because the sons of God are peacemakers and as such they possess the antidote for a culture in crisis.

Checklist for peacemakers:

Peacemakers should be willing to:

- Confront issues of injustice and unrighteousness.
- Become involved.
- Empathise.
- Become vulnerable.
- Allow others to speak their mind and not be threatened by ideas alien to their own.
- Listen and maintain a right attitude.
- See issues from God's perspective.

Peacemaking also involves:

- Being at peace with yourself and God.
- Righteous indignation.
- Reconciliation.
- Negotiation.
- Mediation.
- Intercession.

Notes

[1] Adapted from a story told by Dr Paul Yonggi Cho in *The Fourth Dimension* (Logos, 1979).

[2] John Kennedy, *The Days of the Fathers in Ross-shire* (Christian Focus Publications, 1979).

[3] Bob Mumford, *The King and You* (Revell, 1974).

REDEMPTIVE ATTITUDE No 7

*'Blessed are the peacemakers,
for they will be called
sons of God.'*

'A willingness to position
oneself in the midst of the
conflicts of life and,
from an impartial standpoint,
reconcile man to man
and man to God.'

CHAPTER TEN

POSITIVE I.D.

*'Since Christ had to suffer physically for you,
you must fortify yourselves with the same inner
attitude that he must have had.'*

1 Peter 4:1 [J B PHILLIPS 1960 EDITION]

With a noticeable spring in their step, the two clergymen made their way through the crowded streets of 16th century Oxford. The first man was escorted by the mayor and town alderman, while the second – a close friend and colleague of the first – followed behind.

Turning to his companion behind, the first man enquired if he was heading in the same direction.

'As fast as I can,' he replied.

To the casual observer the cheery words and general behaviour of these two Christians would have meant very little, except when the observer realised that they were both knowingly heading towards an appointment with death. These eminent theologians of their day had been arrested and sentenced to death for their Christian beliefs. Although they were innocent of the charges, they purposefully picked their way through the crowds that lined the pavements to keep their appointment with the executioner.

Death waited and, 'for the joy that was set before them', they hastened to meet it. Not that theirs was to be the relatively quick death of a bullet, a hangman's noose or an electric chair. What faced them were the horrors of the stake, a medieval form of capital punishment in which the victim was publicly stripped and chained to a wooden stake that had been securely fixed in the ground. He or she would then be surrounded by bundles of firewood and forced to suffer the excruciating death of being burned alive.

The two men in question were Hugh Latimer, the Bishop of Worcester, and Nicholas Ridley, the Bishop of London. The year was 1555.

As they arrived at the place of execution, Ridley walked over to where Latimer stood, embraced him and said encouragingly: 'Be of good heart, for God will strengthen us.'

After they refused to take a final opportunity to denounce their Christian beliefs, the order was given to chain both men to a stake and for the funeral pyre to be lit. The wood was piled around each of them, with their persecutors standing by to watch.

As the executioner was about to place a flaming torch at the feet of Ridley, Latimer turned to his friend. 'Be of good comfort, Mr Ridley, and play the man,' he said. 'We shall this day light such a candle, by God's grace, in England as I trust shall never be put out.'

'Blessed – happy, to be envied, and spiritually prosperous . . . are you when people revile you and persecute you and say all kinds of evil things against you falsely on my account. Be glad and supremely joyful, for your reward in heaven is great (strong and intense), for in this same way people persecuted the prophets who were before you' (Matthew 5:11–12 Amplified Bible).

Persecution – a welcome friend

Conflict is inevitable for the Christian. In the midst of immense opposition, Paul and Barnabas sought to strengthen the disciples in Lystra, Iconium and Antioch, 'encouraging them to remain true to the faith' saying: 'We must go through many hardships to enter the kingdom of God' (Acts 14:22).

Paul was well qualified to speak of suffering. His personal catalogue of hardships included such things as imprisonment, severe flogging, exposure to death, five times receiving thirty-nine lashes, beaten with a rod, stoned, shipwrecked, in danger from false brothers and bandits, hungry, thirsty, cold and naked (see 2 Corinthians 11:23–27).

Paul informs the Philippian church that 'it has been granted to you on behalf of Christ not only to believe on him, but also to suffer for him' (Philippians 1:29). He then goes on to parallel their angle of approach to suffering with that of Jesus: 'Have this attitude in yourselves which was also in Christ Jesus' (see Philippians 2:1–11 NASB).

Although some Christians view opposition as negative, the Bible teaches that conflict can be positive. In fact, it would be fair to say that some difficulties are not only natural but, in the long term, beneficial. Paul had a positive attitude to persecution: 'I delight in weaknesses, in insults, in hardships, in persecutions, in difficulties. For when I am weak, then I am strong' (2 Corinthians 12:10).

Opposition, far from being a stranger to Paul, was an expected reaction to righteousness. James, an advocate of the same angle of approach to life, writes: 'When all kinds of trials and temptations crowd into your lives, my brothers, don't resent them as intruders, but welcome them as friends! Realise that they come to test your faith and to produce in you the quality of endurance' (James 1:2–3 J B Phillips).

Life without conflict

In his book *The Time Machine*, H G Wells described an imaginary future very different from our own. It is an environment free from weeds and fungi, where nettles don't sting and the summer evening air is free from mosquitoes. In this seemingly idyllic environment the entire population lives in splendid homes and everyone wears expensive clothes. There is no sign of either social or economic struggle and the necessity for work has been eliminated. Disease has been stamped out and people live in perfect security in an earth where violence is rare.

Yet, in what some might call paradise, Wells observed that the removal of hardship, discomfort, violence, wild beasts and the threat of conflict had produced a weak, insipid, spineless generation. The weak remained weak and the strong had no need of their strength. The result was a society that was physically, intellectually and emotionally crippled.

In such an environment people became idle, easily fatigued, lacking in interest and quickly discouraged. Commenting on this scientific scenario, Wells said: 'We are kept keen on the grindstone of pain and necessity.'

Martin Luther King had his dream, but I have a recurring nightmare. In it I see babies born in Christian hospitals and Christian parents sending children to Christian schools, to learn from Christian teachers and to play with other Christian children. This so-called spiritual Utopia promotes Christian businesses for Christian workers and encourages Christian holidays in Christian theme parks.

I'm not saying that Christian institutions in themselves are wrong. But if such a lifestyle is symptomatic of a ghetto mentality that views the world as a no-go area, then the church is in trouble. If furnishing the household of faith with such luxury items further comforts and consoles an already cocooned Christianity, then 'judgement [must] begin with the family of God' (1 Peter 4:17).

In the same way, if we maintain a homegroup system that plays host to a weekly pity party, that system panders to the immature cries of an 'I want' generation. If we persistently redecorate our man-made structures to cater for in-house needs, we are papering over the cracks of a house with foundational problems. If we pander to the whims and fancies of a smug, self-satisfied people, we are merely rearranging the deckchairs on an ill-fated *Titanic*.

For some people the word 'church' has become synonymous with comfort – a safe haven from the nasty world. Paul, on the other hand, reminds us that 'everyone who wants to live a godly life in Christ Jesus will be persecuted' (2 Timothy 3:12).

Persecution for the righteous is *natural* – it is part of life's process of development. As the botanist watches the emerging caterpillar struggle from its chrysalis, he or she may be tempted to quicken the process by cutting the creature free. But during those moments of struggle a secretion is released that strengthens and prepares the butterfly's wings for flight. So, too, for us Christians. If it were possible for us to be cut free from some confrontational issues, it would deny us a key part of growing up in God.

Persecution is a natural response to right living. It is also *personal*. Those hassles we find difficult to handle are often tailormade to suit us. God forms and administers our troubles so as to fit us exactly. As Bob Mumford put it once: 'God fixes a fix to fix you, and if you unfix the fix before you're fixed, he'll send another fix to fix you.'

One comforting fact is that God also knows our limits and 'will not let you be tempted beyond what you can bear' (1 Corinthians 10:13). Another comforting fact is the knowledge that persecution – whether it is *seasonal*, temporary or frequent – doesn't last for ever, 'though now for a little while you may be distressed by trials and suffer temptations' (1 Peter 1:6 Amplified Bible). The fire, pruning hook, flail and rod are all for our betterment. They are 'tutors and governors' that bring us to maturity (Galatians 4:2 KJV), if we are 'exercised thereby' (Hebrews 12:11 KJV), that is, if we learn the intended lesson from them.

In times of trouble we need to remember that persecution can prove *beneficial*. Conflict can accomplish in us things that blessing never could. 'We know that all things work together for good to them that love God, to them who are the called according to his purpose' (Romans 8:28 KJV). There is a proper conclusion in all pressure, though we may not be able to understand the reason why. Rather than becoming embroiled in the reason for the conflict, we need to align ourselves with the attitude of Christ.

The wine press is an integral part in the process of producing new wine. The crucible is essential for purifying gold. The pruning hook is needed for procuring fruit. In a similar way, persecution is beneficial to us. The attitude of Joshua and Caleb was to view conflict as a means of growing rather than groaning. When faced with literal giants, they said: 'They are bread for us' (Numbers 14:9 KJV). Although Joshua and Caleb were in the minority, they saw the impending conflict as a means of growth and maturity.

Enemy territory

We live in enemy territory. 'We know,' writes John, 'that . . . the whole world is under the control of the evil one' (1 John 5:19). By the 'world' John means the unregenerate inhabitants, who are governed by the devil himself (John 14:30). The material world is not evil of itself; rather, the systems or governments that oversee it are influenced and manipulated by dark spiritual powers (see Ephesians 6:12).

Conversely, the Psalmist declares: 'The earth is the Lord's, and everything in it, the world, and all who live in it' (Psalm 24:1). Like it or not, we're at war. The whole world is involved in a dispute, a question of ownership, an issue of sovereignty. We are either for God and against Satan, or for Satan and against God. Satan is earth's illegal squatter and as such needs to be ousted from the lives of unregenerate people.

God's kingdom and Satan's are diametrically opposed; they are as different as day and night, life and death. Paul expresses this cosmic conflict and its opposing factions in two questions: 'What do righteousness and wickedness have in common? Or what fellowship can light have with darkness?' (see 2 Corinthians 6:14–17).

This world is the theatre of war, and the conflict is an issue of sovereignty. It has been that way since God declared his intention in the Garden of Eden: 'I will put enmity between you and the woman, and between your offspring and hers; he will crush your head, and you will strike his heel' (Genesis 3:15).

Every Christian is a conscript in this battle, for there is no neutrality. Ruth Paxson writes: 'The immediate object in the conflict is the redemption and reconciliation of the human race ruined through sin. The ultimate object is the restoration of God to undivided sovereignty over all his universe; in other words, the rule of the kingdom of God.'[1]

Read the small print!

Drawing his description of Christian character to a close, Jesus begins to put his final touches to the masterpiece. Matthew 5:11–12 re-emphasises verse 10: 'Blessed . . . enviably fortunate and spiritually prosperous [that is, in the state in which one enjoys and finds satisfaction in God's favour and salvation, regardless of his outward conditions], are those who are persecuted for righteousness' sake (for being and doing right), for theirs is the kingdom of heaven' (Amplified Bible).

This eighth attitude, strategically placed as it is, sums up all that has gone before. In effect, what Jesus is saying is: 'When all these Christian characteristics become evident in your life, the result will be persecution, insults, false accusations and people ostracising you.'

In most contracts this kind of clause would be tucked away in the small print so as to not discourage the prospective buyer. But as William Barclay writes: 'One of the outstanding qualities of Jesus was his sheer honesty. He never left men in any doubt what would happen to them if they chose to follow him. He was clear that he had come "not to make life easy, but to make men great".'[2]

Although few of us will ever be called upon to endure the suffering of Ridley and Latimer, our angle of approach to both physical and verbal abuse should follow their example. We are to respond positively to opposition, not react against it. This is an attitude we ignore at our cost. Because the kingdom of God is diametrically opposed to the kingdom of this world – spiritually, morally, ethically and behaviourally – persecution is inevitable. The effect of these eight attitudes working together, therefore, is potential persecution.

Step by step the first three Beatitudes teach us to rely on God. Then, having taken our fill of righteousness, we are prepared to relate to others. But beware, doing right can result in persecution. Dr Martyn Lloyd-Jones writes: 'If you try to imitate Christ, the world will praise you; if you become Christlike it will hate you.'[3]

Sons of the flame

Some people think of Christianity as the 'great escape', a prepaid ticket to heaven in which life is merely a departure lounge. Such an idea is of course wrong. If we invite people to receive Christ without telling them the cost we are not preaching the good news of the kingdom. We are instead giving a watered-down gospel that attracts people on the basis of need, and produces an evangelical subculture that views the world with suspicion.

This ideology says: 'This world is not my home; I'm just a-passing through. And the quicker we get through bandit territory the better!'

At last the church is beginning to emerge, albeit tentatively, from her self-imposed exile. The balance between being in the world and not of it is being addressed. The church is waking up to the truth that heaven's purposes are to be ultimately harmonised with those of earth. An evangelical escape theology is giving way to a true understanding of the gospel of the kingdom.

Bringing in God's rule is costly, and its price cannot be hidden. As Jesus told his followers: 'Any of you who does not give up everything he has cannot be my disciple' (see Luke 14:25–35).

Paul's prayer for the Philippians gives us yet another insight into his attitude to persecution: 'Not having a righteousness of my own that comes from the law, but that which is through faith in Christ – the righteousness that comes from God and is by faith. I want to know Christ and the power of his resurrection and the fellowship of sharing in his sufferings, becoming like him in his death' (Philippians 3:9–10).

'Whatever the cost or the consequences in terms of this life,' says Paul, 'I want to embrace it as Jesus did. I want to be an overcomer and not just to party through life. I want to determine in my heart to bring in God's government whatever the cost!'

Jim Elliot, one of five missionaries martyred in the Ecuador jungle in 1956, displayed the same kind of attitude. During his college days at Wheaton, Illinois, he wrote: '"He makes his ministers a flame of fire." Am I ignitable? God deliver me from the dread asbestos of "other things". Saturate me with the oil of the Spirit that I may be a flame. But flame is transient, often short-lived. Canst thou bear this, my soul – short life? In me there dwells the Spirit of the Great Short-lived, whose zeal for God's house consumed him. "Make me Thy Fuel, Flame of God."'[4]

In his words to Job, Eliphaz made a profound statement on the issue of persecution: 'Man is born to trouble as surely as sparks fly upward' (Job 5:7). The Hebrew word from which we get the English word 'sparks' was translated by one man as 'son of the flame'. What better way is there to characterise the children of God than 'sons of the flame'?

Just like Shadrach, Meshach and Abednego, our stand for

righteousness is likely to elicit either verbal or physical persecution. But we are 'convinced that neither death nor life, neither angels nor demons, neither the present nor the future, nor any powers, neither height nor depth, nor anything else in all creation, will be able to separate us from the love of God that is in Christ Jesus our Lord' (Romans 8:38–39).

Positive identity

You would think that someone who is merciful, pure in heart and a peacemaker would be loved by everyone – but the opposite is true.

Paul, himself a prisoner in Rome, reminds Timothy of a principle of Christian living: 'Persecution is inevitable for those who are determined to live really Christian lives' (2 Timothy 3:12 J B Phillips). The idealist view of Christian living in many people's thinking is a peace-loving, pleasant, unprovocative, easy-going, non-aggressive cruise through the warm waters of life. Nothing could be further from the truth.

Jesus himself said: 'Do not suppose that I have come to bring peace to the earth. I did not come to bring peace, but a sword.' Previously, when commissioning the Twelve, he indicated that 'brother will betray brother to death . . . All men will hate you because of me' (see Matthew 10:21–42). He then went on to refer to the issue of binding the strong man and all that this means (Mark 3:20–30 NASB).

Christianity means warfare, and kingdom life involves conflict. Yet it is a battle with a difference, for we fight in the light of a victory already won. Christians wear the laurels (crowns) of victory without the scars of battle. Jesus has accomplished for us the victory on the beachhead of Calvary. Our job is to mop up various pockets of resistance. Calvary was our D-Day; the second coming of Jesus Christ will be our VE-Day.

How can we maintain a positive attitude to opposition? Is it possible at all that the persecuted can be seen as 'enviably fortunate and spiritually prosperous'?

Since God's declaration of war, his servants have suffered. Abel was persecuted by his brother Cain. Moses suffered the insults of a congregation of two and a half million members. David suffered at the hands of Saul. Elijah suffered, as did Jeremiah.

Daniel 'so distinguished himself . . . by his exceptional qualities' that others 'tried to find grounds for charges against [him] . . . but they were unable to do so . . . because he was trustworthy and neither corrupt nor negligent' (Daniel 6:3–5). Yet he suffered, not for being difficult, but for righteousness' sake. He was oppressed for doing what was right.

The apostles also suffered, not because they were difficult, but simply because they were righteous. Jesus showed us the perfect angle of approach to persecution: 'When they hurled their insults at him, he did not retaliate . . . Instead, he entrusted himself to him who judges justly' (1 Peter 2:23). Read Fox's *Book of Martyrs* and you will see how righteous people suffered at the hands of religious people. The Covenanters, the Protestant Fathers, leaders of the Evangelical Awakening in the eighteenth century and men like Hudson Taylor all suffered, not because they were difficult or objectionable, but because they were living right lives.

The remarkable quality that shines through all these dark episodes is the attitude to affliction of the people concerned. The New Testament continually talks in terms of 'being counted worthy to share in Christ's sufferings'. Paul described this to the Philippians as 'the fellowship of sharing in his sufferings' (Philippians 3:10).

Peter puts it like this: 'Now, dear friends of mine. I beg you not to be unduly alarmed at the fiery ordeals which come to test your faith, as though this were some abnormal experience. You should be glad, because it means that you are sharing in Christ's

sufferings . . . If you are reproached for being Christ's followers, that is a cause for joy, for you can be sure that God's Spirit
of glory is resting upon you. But take care that none of your
number suffers as a murderer, or a thief, a rogue or a busy-body!
If he suffers as a Christian he has nothing to be ashamed of and
may glorify God by confessing Christ's name' (1 Peter 4:12–16
J B Phillips). 'Even if you should suffer for the sake of righteousness, you are blessed' (1 Peter 3:14 NASB).

Why is it a blessing? Because to suffer for righteousness'
sake is to be identified with Jesus. Persecution is viewed in the
New Testament as an association of kind. Jesus follows on from
his discourse on the true vine and its branches by reminding his
disciples: 'If the world hates you, keep in mind that it hated me
first . . . Remember the words I spoke to you: "No servant is
greater then his master." If they persecuted me, they will persecute you also . . . They will treat you this way because of my
name' (John 15:18–21).

Pressures, problems and persecution are all a part of life. Yet
when they are the result of a righteous lifestyle, we can rejoice
because persecution is evidence that we are acting just like
Jesus. The Pharisees hated Jesus because of his absolute holiness. A disciple is expected to be like his master, and the son is
to bear a family resemblance. As sons of God we must therefore
have an attitude that expects opposition. In fact, Jesus warned
his followers: 'Woe to you when all men speak well of you, for
that is how their fathers treated the false prophets' (Luke 6:26).

We can have a positive attitude to persecution when we
realise that the world will hate us, exclude us, insult us and
reject us because we are like Jesus. When we are persecuted for
righteousness' sake it is a sign that the world associates us with
Jesus. The apostles, having been flogged and ordered not to
speak in the name of Jesus, left the Sanhedrin court 'rejoicing
because they had been counted worthy of suffering disgrace for
the Name' (see Acts 5:17–42).

For righteousness' sake!

We are to have a positive attitude to persecution that is 'because of righteousness', not persecution because we are foolish or just difficult to get on with. There is no virtue in being persecuted for the wrong reasons. Peter makes it clear that we must never be persecuted 'as a murderer, or a thief, or any sort of criminal; or as a mischief-maker (a meddler) in the affairs of others – infringing on their rights' (1 Peter 4:15 Amplified Bible).

Such persecution would rarely happen in a local church. But what if we were to classify these charges in another way:

- Murder – Someone who makes an attack on another person's life. This could include the seeds of murder, such as hatred, resentment or the assassination of a person's character. Such are grounds for unjustified suffering.
- Theft – To steal is to abuse a person's possessions. We could therefore say that included in seeds of theft are the stealing of another person's time or the taking of praise due to another.
- Meddle – Interfering in a person's responsibilities; becoming a busy-body. Offering unwise, untimely or unwelcome help.

If we suffer for any of these issues, the persecution that follows is justified and deserved. But if we are 'insulted because of the name of Christ' we should rejoice in that this is an acknowledgement of our state and standing in Christ. We are therefore provoked to rejoice that we 'bear that name' (1 Peter 4:14–16). It is this issue of positive identification that makes for a positive approach to persecution.

There are degrees of persecution. The Oxford Dictionary defines 'persecute' as 'pursue with enmity and ill-treatment; harass; worry; importune'. Such harassment may range from verbal to emotional abuse and may also extend to physical abuse of one's property or person.

Some Christians today are imprisoned for their faith. Others are ostracised by their peers, colleagues, family or relatives. But for the majority of Christians in the West the persecution is of a verbal nature: insults, false rumours, gossip, slander and libel.

The Greek word *dioko*, translated 'persecution', means 'to put to flight, drive away, to pursue,' says Vine. Kittel suggests a twofold idea: first, that of 'to ride', 'to march', 'to set in rapid motion'; and second, 'to expel', 'to accuse'. This is seen in the words of Pharaoh pursuing the children of Israel: 'The enemy boasted, "I will pursue, I will overtake them. I will divide the spoils; I will gorge myself on them. I will draw my sword and my hand will destroy them"' (Exodus 15:9). Such situations are the result of a clash of the kingdoms.[5]

Taking various versions of Luke 6:22, we know that the world will 'despise and hate us, exclude and excommunicate us (as disreputable), slander us and reject all that we stand for, because you are loyal to the Son of Man' (Amplified and J B Phillips).

Kingdom living involves conflict. But approached correctly, such persecution can be a means of rejoicing. We are not to allow resentment or a desire for retaliation to take root. Instead, we are to 'be glad . . . and jump for joy – your reward in heaven is magnificent. For that is exactly how their fathers treated the prophets' (Luke 6:23 J B Phillips).

Numbers clearly are significant to God. In biblical numerology, the number seven is the number of completion or perfection, while eight is the number of new beginnings. If this teaching is true, this eighth attitude could be said to speak of the beginning of a new era. This attitude, climaxing all that has gone before, has to do with our angle of approach to pressure.

Richard Wurmbrand was held for fourteen years in Communist prisons. For almost three years he was kept in a room three paces by three, thirty-five feet under the ground, with only a tube for air. Despite being beaten, tortured and drugged, his captors could not break this man of God and force him to confess to the false allegations brought against him.

He writes of his awful persecution: 'The Communists believe that happiness comes from material satisfaction; but alone in my cell, cold, hungry and in rags, I danced for joy every night . . . Sometimes I was so filled with joy that I felt I would burst if I did not give it expression. I remembered the words of Jesus: "Blessed are you when men come to hate you, when they exclude you from their company and reproach you and cast out your name as evil on account of the Son of Man. Rejoice in that day and leap for joy!" I told myself: "I've carried out only half this command. I've rejoiced, but that is not enough. Jesus says clearly that we must also leap."

'When next the guard peered through the spy-hole, he saw me springing about my cell. His orders must have been to distract anyone who showed signs of breakdown, for he padded off and returned with some food from the staff room: a hunk of bread, some cheese and sugar. As I took them I remembered how the verse in St Luke went on: "Rejoice in that day and leap for joy – for behold your reward is great." It was a very large piece of bread: more than a week's ration.

'I rarely allowed a night to pass without dancing, from then on, although I was never paid for it again. I made up songs and sang them softly to myself and danced to my own music . . . It was a manifestation of joy like the dance of David, a holy sacrifice offered before the altar of the Lord. I did not mind if my captors thought I was mad, for I had discovered a beauty in Christ which I had not known before.

'Sometimes I saw visions . . . Then the cell was full of light . . . Another night I became aware of a great throng of angels moving slowly through the darkness towards my bed. As they approached they sang a song of love.'[6]

If only this could be our attitude to the pressures of life – to have this kind of mind-set when approaching those who ostracise us, or abuse us verbally or physically. Surely what the enemy meant for bad would then be turned to our advantage.

Pure gold

Perhaps the best-documented example of pressure, trials and testing is the story of Job. In his most arduous moment he cried: 'He knows the way that I take; when he has tested me, I shall come forth as gold' (Job 23:10).

God uses only pure gold that has been refined in the fire (Revelation 3:18). Although our redemption is complete, and an internal change has taken place, we still have the dross of wrong thinking, etc, to bring to the surface and skim off. For centuries people have been trying to make gold from lead, but without success. The reason is that there has to be a change in the molecular structure. Our molecular structure has been changed at the cross, but the heat of trials and other pressures brings to the surface the negative as well as the positive.

It is reckoned by most goldsmiths that beaten gold is not only stronger but also of greater value than poured gold. Interestingly, most of the golden instruments in the Tabernacle of Moses were made from beaten gold.

Our attitude needs to be: 'I must be precious and useful if God is allowing me to go through this fiery trial.' Remember that God never leaves his children to go through the fire alone; he is always there with them. He has a vested interest in the gold.

Every obstacle is an opportunity

Adversity can mean success to those who maintain a redemptive, rather than adversarial attitude. John Bunyan wrote *Pilgrim's Progress* in Bedford jail. Luther translated the Bible while confined in Warburg castle. Beethoven was almost totally deaf and burdened with sorrow when he produced his greatest works. Be it the cave, wilderness, pit or prison, it is difficult to find a well-known bible character who did not first have to attend the school of persecution before emerging as a great leader.

In *Awake, My Heart*, Sidlow Baxter writes, 'What is the difference between an obstacle and an opportunity? Our attitude toward it. Every opportunity has a difficulty and every difficulty has an opportunity.'[7]

Notes

[1] Ruth Paxson, *Life on the Highest Plane* (Moody Press, 1928).
[2] Barclay, *The Daily Study Bible* (St Andrew's Press, 1976).
[3] Lloyd-Jones, *Studies in the Sermon on the Mount* (IVP, 1971).
[4] Elisabeth Elliot, *Through Gates of Splendour* (STL, 1980).
[5] Kittel, Vol 2, pp 229–230.
[6] Richard Wurmbrand, *In God's Underground* (WH Allen, 1968).
[7] J Sidlow Baxter, *Awake, My Heart* (Zondervan, 1960).

REDEMPTIVE ATTITUDE No 8

'Blessed are those who are persecuted because of righteousness, for theirs is the kingdom of heaven.'

'A redemptive approach to pressure, insults and persecution that reacts positively to a recognition that we are living Christlike lives.'

CHAPTER ELEVEN

YOUR KINGDOM COME

'Be careful how you think; your life is shaped by your thoughts.'

Proverbs 4:23 [GOOD NEWS BIBLE]

If you slice through the cake of media rhetoric served up to us daily on TV and in newspapers, you will see that we are living in a world in crisis. Across the nations people are reaching their ultimate frustration point where everything they trusted in is beginning to crumble.

God is shaking the shakeable in order to establish the unshakeable. The writer to the Hebrews puts it this way: '"Once more I will shake not only the earth but also the heavens." The words "once more" indicate the removing of what can be shaken – that is, created things – so that what cannot be shaken may remain. Therefore, since we are receiving a kingdom that cannot be shaken, let us be thankful, and so worship God acceptably with reverence and awe' (Hebrews 12:26–28).

As the world's economic, political and social structures begin to weaken, the church cannot afford to be sidetracked. The church has been chosen to implement a divine government that cannot be shaken. She is the principal player in the theatre of world events.

What, then, is the church? According to John Bright: 'The New Testament understood her simply as the true Israel, God's covenant and servant people, called to exhibit the righteousness of his kingdom before the world, charged with proclaiming that kingdom in the world and summoning men to its covenant fellowship. To that church are all the promises given. And that is the church that we are called to be.'[1]

Neither the mental ascent of a bona fide pew filler, or the

empty platitudes of a professional Christian, are sufficient for the task at hand. The challenge facing today's church is for a people who are spiritually aggressive. God is looking for a people who, rather than spectate, choose to participate, to lay hold of what God first laid hold of them (Philippians 3:12). Matthew refers to 'the kingdom of heaven . . . forcefully advancing, and forceful men lay hold of it' (Matthew 11:12).

The church, as heaven's elect representative on earth, is where God's will is carried out without interference. God's kingdom is 'his kingship, his rule, his authority, his sway, his reign in our lives'. As God's redeemed people we are commissioned to be the forerunners of heaven's rule on earth. We must rally to the call and become 'an administration suitable to the fullness of the times' (Ephesians 1:10 NASB).

God wants heroes

We are witnessing the disintegration of a culture that has abandoned Judeo-Christian values. In this culture we need not apologise for our convictions on marriage, sexuality, the sanctity of life and the absolute truths of God's Word. God is raising up an alternative society with spiritual backbone. He is looking for heroes – disciples who refuse to conform to a religious lifestyle that restricts them from pursuing God's purposes.

An attitude of individualism that promotes isolation and independence is wrong. Yet each of us needs room to express our originality and creativity. As someone has said: 'All people are born originals, though most of us will die copies.' In some Christian circles the pressure is on to conform to a man-made idealism. This is not only squeezing the lifeblood out of the church but incarcerating people in a prison of religious routine. If we have an environment that fails to appreciate and accept the many-faceted grace of God in person, we will ultimately produce a community that is both bland and boring.

Heroes also choose to assert their divinity in the face of their humanity. They refuse to let human weakness and circumstances hamper them. They are determined to overcome life's dilemmas and accomplish great things for God. They draw on the indwelling power of the Holy Spirit and aggressively pursue their God-given destiny, refusing to be sidetracked by anyone or anything.

We live in an environment of compromise. But the Christian has to decide whether or not he or she is going to be silenced by the pressure to conform, or rise above the tide of popular opinion and dare to be different. Heroes display the kind of lifestyle that is different – so different that it demands an explanation. They have an outstanding character; by exerting a godly influence, they overcome obstacles to stamp their mark on the world around them.

A captive audience

Jesus announced his arrival on the stage of world events with the words: 'Repent, for the kingdom of heaven is near' (Matthew 4:17). This opening gambit was guaranteed to attract a crowd. His words were like music to Jewish ears as they heralded – hopefully – the dawning of a new era.

The fact that the Jews lived under Roman domination and pagan rule only served to heighten their level of expectation of a coming deliverer. The Jewish nation, locked into this powerful political system, longed for its overthrow and the restoration of God's rule. In Jesus the kingdom of God had come, but not in a way that the majority of Jews had anticipated. Nevertheless, it had arrived.

Jesus didn't come representing a kingdom of geographical boundaries or international borders. He came to institute a rule that would ultimately embrace everything his heavenly Father had created.

Although Jesus said his kingdom was not 'of this world', he still maintained that it was to be 'in the world'. In simple terms, Jesus was spelling out the truth that God's kingdom is unique. It has not come to promote the standards, behavioural patterns or business procedures of this present age. Neither is it an ethereal pie-in-the-sky rule reserved for an age to come. The kingdom of God is here and now – a present reality.

Like a catalyst of cosmic proportions, God's kingdom is our only hope of returning to heaven's eternal game plan. God's government is unshakeable in its character and supernatural in its conception (1 Corinthians 15:50). It is poised to infiltrate every stratum of secular society. In doing so the gospel of the kingdom will oppose people's futile attempts to rule without God. It will bring all things into subjection to Christ, thus uniting discordant humanity with a holy, righteous God.

Ordaining the Twelve

'When he saw the crowds, he went up on a mountainside and sat down. His disciples came to him, and he began to teach them' (Matthew 5:1).

Having chosen the twelve disciples, Jesus began to piece together his manifesto. The Sermon on the Mount, possibly a collection of teachings given over a period of time, represents a summary of all Jesus taught his disciples.

If these teachings were to assist Jesus in establishing God's rule on earth, the people would need to understand his strategy. That's why Luke's account places this sermon directly after the choosing of the Twelve (Luke 6:13). Someone has in fact called the Sermon on the Mount 'The Ordination Address to the Twelve'.

The Sermon on the Mount is the charge given by Jesus to his fellow ministers. It is the heart of a Master to his disciples, the official teaching Jesus shared with his inner circle of followers.

As if to illustrate this, Matthew introduces this sermon by making it clear that Jesus withdrew from the crowd, went up the mountainside and 'sat down' to teach. When a Jewish rabbi gave general teaching, he would either stand or walk about. But when he chose to give the official teaching on an issue, the rabbi would always be seated.

Matthew 5–7 is, therefore, the epitome of all Jesus taught concerning character and conduct. It is a compendium of thoughts that show us the frame of mind Jesus wants his followers to have.

The subject of redemptive attitudes was a preparation for all Jesus taught concerning Christian living. In describing these eight keys to success, Jesus defined the kind of lifestyle that receives God's applause. We could paraphrase each attitude with the words: 'Blessed, to be admired, envied, congratulated and imitated are those who practise this angle of approach to life.'

In talking about these attitudes, Jesus showed his disciples the kind of perspective on life he wanted them to have. He defined the mental lenses vital for success.

In his book *See You at the Top*, Zig Ziglar writes: 'Attitude is much more important than your aptitude. Despite the overwhelming evidence which supports the importance of the right mental attitude, our entire educational system from kindergarten through graduate school virtually ignores or is unaware of this factor in our life. 90% of our education is directed at acquiring facts and figures with only 10% of our education aimed at our "feelings" or attitudes.

'These figures are truly incredible and distressing when we realise that our "thinking" [facts] brain is only 10% as large as our "feelings" [emotion-attitude] brain.

'A study by Harvard University revealed that 85% of the reason for success, accomplishments, promotion, etc, were because of our attitudes and only 15% because of our technical expertise . . . We can alter our lives by altering our attitudes.'[2]

Jesus made attitudes fundamental to discipleship.

God's original intention

Genesis gives us what could be called 'God's original declaration of intention'. The divine dialogue reads: 'Let us make man in our image, in our likeness, and let them rule over the fish of the sea and the birds of the air, over the livestock, over all the earth, and over all the creatures that move along the ground' (Genesis 1:26). Taking various translations, Genesis 1:26–28 presents us with such key words as 'image' and 'likeness', 'rule' and 'dominion'.

There has been considerable debate over the words 'image' and 'likeness'. It is sufficient to say that both expressions are to do with people's character, while 'rule' and 'dominion' have to do with their commission or call (which in turn results in conflict). Priority is given to character. Once God had made men and women in his image and likeness, he commissioned them to maintain and extend heaven's rule on earth.

As heaven's viceroys, Adam and Eve were to bring all creation under God's governmental rule. Earth's order was to be a reflection of heaven's. Jesus taught his disciples: 'Our Father in heaven, hallowed be your name, your kingdom come, your will be done on earth as it is in heaven' (Matthew 6:9–10). While the first Adam failed to fulfil his commission, the last Adam, Jesus (1 Corinthians 15:45), was successful.

'Image', together with its partner, 'likeness', is the result of a divine work of grace in an individual. Irenaeus suggests that when man was first created he 'was not what he finally would be, but that his destiny was to advance from glory to glory, and that, even if there had been no Fall, the end was designed to be even more splendid than the beginning'.

Whatever our understanding of the Hebrew language, God's original declaration of intention clearly put character before call or commission. Through Christ's redemptive work, God has re-established the means by which his original declaration of intention can be fulfilled in humankind. New birth has made us 'partakers of the divine nature' (2 Peter 1:4 NASB). It has enabled us to fulfil the purpose for which we were predestined, that is, 'to be conformed to the likeness of [God's] Son' (Romans 8:29), and to 'go and make disciples of all nations' (Matthew 28:18–19).

In this way those who by grace are related to the last Adam, Jesus, extend God's rule on earth.

Character or charisma

New birth invests God's nature in us. That nature develops to form God's likeness in us more perfectly. Put another way, new birth makes me God's child with all the potential of sonship (2 Peter 1:3). Sonship is to do with maturity of character and ability to take charge. After all, you have never seen a shop with the title W H Smith & Child; it always reads W H Smith & Son. Maturity is the means by which a son is given the responsibility to manage a portion of his father's estate.

Parents well understand that giving birth is a relatively quick event compared with the time taken in bringing that same child to maturity and adulthood. Jesus, having called his disciples to follow him, was concerned to bring them to a place of maturity. He invested in them so that they would have a right perspective on life to handle power and authority. 'When Jesus had called the Twelve together, he gave them power and authority to drive out all demons and to cure diseases, and he sent them out to preach the kingdom of God and to heal the sick' (Luke 9:1–2).

The Greek word translated 'character' has the basic meaning as 'to notch or emboss'. The idea conveyed is that of a skilled craftsman working on some basic material to create a thing of beauty and amazement. Through the indwelling Holy Spirit we 'are being transformed into (Jesus') likeness with ever-increasing glory, which comes from the Lord, who is the Spirit' (2 Corinthians 3:18).

We are called first and foremost to mirror the likeness of Jesus. We are also commissioned to oust the illegal squatter, Satan, and to bring back King Jesus. T O Chisholm's old hymn puts it:

> *O to be like thee, blessed Redeemer,*
> *This is my constant longing and prayer;*
> *Gladly I'll forfeit all of earth's resource,*
> *Jesus, thy perfect likeness to wear.*
>
> *O to be like thee,*
> *O to be like thee,*
> *Blessed Redeemer, pure as thou art;*
> *Come in thy sweetness,*
> *Come in thy fulness:*
> *Stamp thine own image deep on my heart.*

Talent, natural ability and strong personality might promote the person, but only a balance between character and charisma (gift) will adequately promote God's purposes. While your gift might open doors, a character deficiency will certainly close them. God will take charge of the breadth of our ministry, if we take responsibility for its depth.

Godly character is vital

If our generation is to bring back the King, godly character will be vital. John the Baptist prepared the way for Christ's first coming; the church will herald his second.

The prophet Isaiah foresaw John's ministry as 'a voice of one calling: "In the desert prepare the way for the Lord; make straight in the wilderness a highway for our God. Every valley shall be raised up, every mountain and hill made low; the rough ground shall become level, the rugged places a plain. And the glory of the Lord will be revealed, and all mankind together will see it"' (Isaiah 40:3–5; also Matthew 3:3; John 1:23).

Like the inhabitants of a remote town preparing for the visit of an important dignitary, we are called to prepare the approaches to the town in readiness for the visit of the King of kings:

- We are to fill in those valleys of unsociability, discourtesy and indiscipline, the lack of character qualities.
- We need to level off the hills of anger, pride, those aspects of our life that are unpleasant and make life hard work.
- We are to smooth and straighten any rough areas of abrasiveness or crooked ways of unrighteous behaviour.

Then, through us, the King can be seen in all his glory and win the admiration he so deserves. By making character a priority, the church will set the agenda for the King's return.

In an age when so much emphasis is placed on gift and personality, we would do well to remember the advice given to the prophet Samuel. Saul, having lost his right to exercise authority because of a wrong attitude, was about to be replaced by David, a man after God's own heart. Before the anointing oil touched the lad's head, God gave his prerequisite for power: 'The Lord does not look at the things man looks at. Man looks at the outward appearance, but the Lord looks at the heart' (1 Samuel 16:7).

The church of today would do well to remind herself that in the garden and on the mountainside God placed his priority on character before charisma.

My nine-year-old son may have the physical strength to hold

a chainsaw. But as yet he doesn't have the maturity to handle either the power or responsibility that goes with using such machinery. Although we all want to handle the power and authority involved in sonship, each of us has first to make sure that our character is able to cope.

Today engineers are able to manufacture the metal casing for so-called 'super-guns' – cannons that can fire shells many miles. The question is not if the gun will fire, but can it cope with the recoil? The kickback could damage the gun so severely that it would become useless. If the Christian church continues to load considerable responsibility, authority and scope on untried leaders, the recoil of fame and fortune will continue to shatter their lives. This will leave in its wake a debris of broken marriages and divided churches.

James Fisher, a well-known and widely-travelled psychiatrist, went throughout the world looking for the positive qualities that make for good mental health. He said: 'I dreamed of writing a handbook that would be simple, practical, easy to understand and easy to follow; it would tell people how to live – what thoughts and attitudes and philosophies to cultivate, and what pitfalls to avoid in seeking mental health. And quite by accident I discovered that such a work had been completed – the Beatitudes.'[3]

Do you want to discover the winning edge, the biblical approach to people, objects and events? Then a redemptive attitude is the answer. The fact is, we can alter our lives by altering our attitudes.

Notes

[1] John Bright, *The Kingdom of God* (Abingdon Press, 1979).
[2] Zig Ziglar, *See You at the Top* (Baptist Spanish Publishing House, 1982).
[3] Neil Warren & Marie Jahoda, *Attitudes* (Penguin, 1966).

CONCLUSION

Imagine . . . Just for a minute let your imagination run free. There you are sitting at home relaxing after a busy day at work. The doorbell rings. Wearily you make your way to see who it is.

As you open the front door there stands a smartly-dressed businessman who introduces himself as representing a firm of London solicitors.

'Is your name Mr . . . ?' To your surprise he knows your name.

'Yes,' you reply, becoming more inquisitive by the minute.

'Please excuse the questions, but I represent an American client who's looking for a distant relative.'

'Oh, yes.'

'Did your mother come from Ireland?' he continues with the efficient tones of a well-educated man.

The answer is 'yes' again.

What can this man want from you? As you search his face for clues, your mind presses the rewind button to rerun your life so far. But before you can begin to review the episodes of your life, the stranger asks another question.

'Did she have a brother who went to America in the mid 1880s?'

'Look, why not come in? We've got a family Bible and our family history's all written down.'

Retrieving the large volume from the attic and removing the dust, you outline the family tree.

'There's my mother. She was born in Belfast. She had four

brothers, one of whom emigrated to New York. But we haven't heard from that side of the family for years.'

'This is wonderful news,' exclaims the solicitor excitedly, who by now is comfortably seated with a cup of tea in his hand. 'You see, tonight ends for me a very long search. You are the last link in the chain. Let me explain. Your uncle went to America and became a very successful property tycoon. He had a son who he left all his money to. Unfortunately, the son died and didn't leave an heir. The lawyers in America have traced his family back to Ireland, and the Irish people have traced it over here. Hence my visit this evening. We have now every reason to believe you to be your uncle's only remaining relative.'

'Would you like another cup of tea? A biscuit?' you inquire.

'No, I'm fine, thank you. I'm pleased to inform you that, based on what you've shown me this evening, you're the sole benefactor of a very large inheritance.'

Your mind, bursting with excitement, begins to race.

I can buy that new car I've always wanted. Pay off the mortgage on the house. Go to the Bahamas . . .

'At last!' shouts one of the children, who has been bursting to say something all through the conversation. 'Dad, perhaps we can afford to go to Disneyland.'

'No,' says the lawyer, 'you don't understand. Your uncle owned a large number of properties and land.'

'Disneyland here we come!' shouts the eldest child.

'No, I'm sorry to labour the fact, but you still don't seem to understand. They found oil and gold on your uncle's land. We're talking a great deal of money here. Now, of course, it's going to take some time for the courts to finalise all this. But on the basis of what you've furnished me with this evening, if you'd like to call into my office in a week's time I'll be able to give you a small down payment on the inheritance.'

Trying not to be to pushy, you ask in a relaxed voice: 'Er, can you tell us what that first payment would be?'

'Oh, yes, we're talking around £10,000.'

Can you imagine how you would feel? No matter what your mental state of mind up to the moment the doorbell rang, your whole mind-set would suddenly change. Yesterday's problems would fade into insignificance. The future would seem so full of exciting possibilities. Suddenly, you are bursting with enthusiasm; your expectation levels have risen. In fact, your whole perspective on life has changed. You are now able to face the pressures of life with a totally new outlook.

What has happened? You haven't received a penny of your promised inheritance, but you have taken on a whole new set of beliefs. These have affected the way you feel, which in turn is changing the way you behave. You have altered your whole approach to life by realigning your attitude.

If allowed, the truth contained in this book, appropriated aright, will make you a spiritual millionaire. No matter what comes your way – be it positive or negative – your angle of approach to life will be redemptive.

As you are consumed by God's purpose for your life you will look every day for ways to turn life into a win-win situation.

You can then choose to be a winner who sometimes loses, rather than a loser who sometimes wins.

Chris Spicer conducts teaching seminars on a variety of Christian subjects. For those interested please write to:

4th Base Ministries
PO Box 107
Birmingham
B30 1DF